Mr. Rigi

MW00897352

(...or is it "I")

by

Marsha Honeycutt Marcela

The George Rigney we all remember.

Dedication

This book is dedicated to the many, many students who were lucky enough to have Mr. Rigney as their English teacher.

"Go rest high on that mountain.

Son, your work on earth is done."

Vince Gill

George Rigney's school portrait taken his first year of teaching after earning his official teaching license at Radford University.

Contents

Acknowledgments

Given that this is my first attempt at writing a book, I am very grateful to Laurel Hill Publishing Company for agreeing to publish my book as well as agreeing to donate its part of the profits to the George Daniel Rigney Memorial Scholarship Fund. Tom Perry's assistance with this project will not be forgotten.

I am also grateful to my boys, Braxton and Rigney Marcela, for their written contribution. I will be forever proud of their devotion to Mr. Rigney and the time they spent with him. Rigney's special bond with him became a highlight of Mr. Rigney's life during his final years, and the visits were greatly anticipated and appreciated. Rigney's teaching career and Braxton's academic achievements and law degree were all sources of pride for Mr. Rigney. May Mr. Rigney's love of teaching live on through Rigney.

To my husband, Mike, who never complained about the time I spent with Mr. Rigney, I am very appreciative. He took care of the home front while I traveled to Carroll and Patrick Counties with Mr. Rigney.

Thanks to Phyllis Eastridge, Bruce Dollarhite, and the Guidance Department at Patrick County High School for their work with the Rigney Scholarship Fund.

, A special thanks to Mr. Rigney's family for always allowing me to be part of his life without question.

Without these people, I would have no story.

George Rigney's very first school portrait after becoming a teacher. He was 18 years old.

Prologue

Ralph Waldo Emerson once said, "Few people know how to take a walk. The qualifications are endurance, plain clothes, old shoes, an eye for nature, good humor, vast curiosity, good speech, good silence, and nothing too much." Having taken a few good walks when I was a young girl, I agree with Emerson's prescription, but I think he may have left out one very important component: a knowledgeable friend who can navigate through nature and educate you along the way. For me, that person was Mr. George Rigney, a retired English teacher from Patrick County High School in Stuart, Virginia, where I began my career as an English teacher in August 1984. Mr. Rigney continues to be a legend in Patrick County because during his forty-nine years of teaching, he positively impacted the lives of so many people in Patrick and Carroll Counties in Virginia and Surry County in North Carolina.

It wasn't until the second half of my first year of teaching that I came to know Mr. Rigney. As I became acclimated to my teaching position and colleagues, I became increasingly intrigued by the seemingly endless time and attention he gave to his students. It was never unusual to see him surrounded by a group of five or more students who just wanted to laugh and joke around with him before the beginning of their academic day. He always had time, or at least made time, for them as he rightfully deemed that his purpose for being in a high school. His attention to students didn't stop with their graduations, however, as former students arrived regularly for visits, requests for college/job references, or opportunities to thank him for some remembered favor that had made a difference in their lives.

When I taught with him the summer following my first year of teaching, we began what was to become a true, lifelong friendship. During this short six-week summer session, he taught me the art of teaching to all grades and populations so that my teaching resume includes teaching skills at all grade levels ranging from low-functioning kindergartners with disabilities to Advanced Placement seniors. Little did I know at the time that it would not be the formal training I received at Appalachian State University that would shape my teaching career, but Mr. Rigney's mentoring and daily guidance that would allow me to successfully meet challenges in rural, suburban, and metropolitan academic situations.

Early in my second year of teaching, as my friendship with Mr. Rigney continued to grow, he invited me to his home deep in the mountains of Carroll County, Virginia. I was only twenty-four years old at the time and unaware of how our visit would unfold.

As I drove along a dusty narrow road, I was fairly certain that I would soon drive off the earth into an unknown abyss, but eventually, I saw him and his pet wolf standing by a gate awaiting my arrival. I was expecting him to show me, from afar, the scenic mountain views surrounding his home, so I was surely surprised when he pressed down on a barbed wire fence and told me to cross it. As I gently gathered the bottom of my preppy denim skirt and lifted my leg across that fence, I began the first of what would fill many Sunday afternoons of climbing mountains and walking rugged trails with Mr. Rigney.

The monogrammed sweater and penny loafers I was wearing that day revealed that I was not, and still am not, the outdoorsy type. However, I enjoyed my lessons about nature and mountain life and came to understand what Henry David Thoreau and Ralph Waldo Emerson meant by "transcendentalism," a concept I had never really applied to my own life.

As we stood on a hill and looked across the mountain, Mr. Rigney pointed across the way to a spot "where the snow doesn't melt until May." I drank crystal clear water from a mountain stream using a dipper that was left there permanently for that purpose. We walked around the vacant properties that are today decorated with expensive, beautiful, summer homes. Mr. Rigney had even built a small pier, which allowed me to walk out over the crystal clear water of a nearby lake. We were always accompanied by Brownie, his wolf, who seemed to know the mountain trails readily without prompting.

Over time, Mr. Rigney and I would spend numerous afternoons together. In addition to these routine hikes (for which I quickly learned the proper dress), we would sometimes take a car ride to various places where he had taught in his early career before coming to Patrick County in 1967. Although we didn't visit these locations in chronological order, I would eventually see many of the abandoned structures of the schools where he had taught.

The first such visit, and my favorite school, was a seemingly abandoned shell of a large, one-room, hay-filled building that had once served as Turner School in Carroll County. Mr. Rigney identified that building as where he began his second teaching assignment that started in 1951 when he was nineteen years old. We climbed a steep hill, and he took me inside as he pointed out several spots of interest, including where the pot-bellied stove had once stood, a structure where Mr. Rigney remembered his students hanging their coats, and the corner where he took

the boys to cut their hair. He even showed me the point in the room where

he took students when they needed a spanking. This experience brought

to life the history of rural, mountain education that I had read about but

had never seen or felt. He stayed in this teaching position for only one

year before moving to a two-room school the following year.

While not as enlightening as the actual one-room school, we next

visited Blue Ridge School, which was a white church similar to the one

the Ingalls children attended on the *Little House on the Prairie* television

series. This church was the location of his first teaching assignment.

Worship services were held in the church on Sunday mornings, and school

sessions were held during the week. We weren't able to go inside the

church because it is now used solely for church services and remains

locked. Mr. Rigney was eighteen years old when he started this

assignment at Blue Ridge School.

He had never graduated from high school himself but passed the

Virginia High School Completion Exam that allowed him to receive a

diploma from the Commonwealth of Virginia, permitting him to teach at

this unaccredited school in 1949. While teaching at Blue Ridge, Mr.

Rigney earned $100 per month for teaching forty-eight students in different grades. He stayed one year in this position before accepting an assignment at Turner School, where he had taken me first.

Mr. Rigney never took me to the location of his third teaching position at Snake Creek, because it is probably not in existence today. He described it as a two-room school with two teachers. He taught the twenty-five students with the lowest academic skills in one room for one year. At the close of the year at Snake Creek School, he began the long road through formal education by catching rides to Radford College with other prospective teachers, paying them one dollar per day for the rides. He attended college each summer for the next ten years, working toward a license to teach in accredited schools.

In the process of earning his degrees, Mr. Rigney taught in a variety of schools. Five of the ten years were spent at Pilot View School at Groundhog Mountain, another one-room school. While teaching in unaccredited schools, this five-year tenure would be his lengthiest assignment before the receipt of his teaching license. At the close of these five years, he would move to the Dewey School, another one-room school, where he taught for a year.

Mr. Rigney completed the requirements for his license in 1962 while teaching at Round Knob School on the Carroll and Wythe County line, where he stayed for four years. Upon receipt of his license, he was then encouraged by Dr. Howard of Radford College to enroll in three more summer sessions to earn the highest teacher's certificate awarded at that time in the state of Virginia. As a result, in 1963, Mr. Rigney enrolled in the Teacher Training Program at McGuffey Hall, managed by Radford College, but affiliated with Virginia Polytechnical Institute and University.

Mr. Rigney fondly recalled the details of McGuffey Hall as both very professional and intended mostly for women. To demonstrate the differences that time has made in the field of education, he reported that married women could not be hired for the McGuffey Teacher Training School. While completing this program, Mr. Rigney had many professional decisions to make as Dr. Martin, President of Radford College, encouraged him to study special education on a full scholarship. On the other hand, his friend and mentor, Ms. Bennett, stressed the importance of studying for a master's degree. In the meantime, he accepted an assignment to student teach in a sixth-grade class and then followed Dr. Howard's previous advice to get fully certified to teach in an elementary school foregoing the scholarship to study special education.

Once licensed to teach in an accredited school, he accepted a position at St. Paul School in Carroll County, Virginia, where he started as a handwriting teacher under the supervision of Principal Joe Berry. Even as he aged, Mr. Rigney's handwriting continued to be close to perfect.

After one year, he took his teaching talents south when he accepted a position as a fifth-grade teacher at Flat Rock Elementary School in Mount Airy, North Carolina, in 1965, the same year he earned his master's degree from Radford College.

I take great pleasure in the fact that Mr. Rigney taught at Flat Rock Elementary School the same year I entered there as a first-grader. Although I was only six years old and would not, at that time, have known or recognized what an extraordinary teacher he was, our paths just missed crossing at that point.

My sister attended Flat Rock during the two years Mr. Rigney was there and remembered him as a staff member although she did not have him as a teacher. He was replaced at Flat Rock by the man who would eventually be my sixth, seventh, and eighth grade grammar teacher.

After leaving Flat Rock Elementary in 1967, Mr. Rigney returned to Virginia, where he accepted a job at Stuart High School, marking the beginning of his thirty-three-year career in Patrick County, Virginia. He taught at Stuart High for only three years, after which the local schools consolidated into what is now known as Patrick County High School. In

1970, he participated in the opening of this new high school, where he stayed for the remainder of his teaching career.

Many of those years were spent under the supervision of Principal James K. Hiatt, who remembers him fondly as "a teacher with great concern for his students both before and after their graduation." He was named Teacher of the Year for Patrick County in 1973 by student vote. He kept the newspaper article framed and on his wall until his death in 2018. He said, "I was flying high in those days."

During his thirty years in the Patrick County School District, Mr. Rigney taught English in grades eight through twelve to students at all academic levels. He was always one of the last people whom students and teachers saw at the end of the day as he had parking lot duty. He was also one of the sponsors of a group of students who performed one-act plays traveling regularly with them to performances. Mr. Rigney was the announcer for the annual spelling bee, but the thing I remember most was his announcement of the names of the boys at the commencement ceremonies. He enunciated each syllable of the student's name, adding dignity and reverence to that name.

Another fond memory was the day a rock and roll band came to our school and asked Mr. Rigney to come on stage and lip-sync to "Rock and Roll All Night." He swayed his hips and went along with the event creating laughter and enjoyment for those watching.

He truly had a rapport with all students with whom he came in contact, many of whom he didn't even teach. He never differentiated among race, gender, or social class of his students, but treated them all with the respect that led them back to him after their graduation. He has taught young people who became doctors, lawyers, teachers, inmates, factory workers, retail workers, and countless people from other walks of life.

In 1989, Mr. Rigney was listed as one of the top sixty-four teachers in the United States by *Newsweek* magazine. He was nominated by a former student, David Ratliff, who had returned to Patrick County High School as a history teacher. The county was delighted when his name appeared in *Newsweek,* prompting the publication of a story outlining some of his educational history in the local newspapers.

The Sallie Mae Foundation and *Newsweek* honored Mr. Rigney with a plaque for his contributions to teaching. That plaque now hangs on the wall of Rigney Marcela's home in Cornelius, North Carolina, as Mr. Rigney gave it to him as a gift when he graduated from Western Carolina University with his teaching degree.

It is for all of these reasons that out of deep respect for Mr. Rigney, I named my son, "Rigney," after my mentor and friend. While a student in a suburban high school and now a teacher in an elementary school in the same area, he wears the name proudly as no one else there shares it with him. He now goes by Rigney or Mr. Marcela. I knew of no better way that I could convey how very much Mr. Rigney has meant to me throughout the years of my teaching career. I will always remember his generous contributions to young people—especially to me. I try to follow his example.

After Mr. Rigney's retirement in 1999, I visited him in the mountains. I didn't always find him, but I left notes in his mailbox to let him know that I had been there. I sent cards for all holidays, including Father's Day, but I missed the face-to-face contact that I enjoyed during our many days of teaching together.

It would be extreme circumstances that brought him fully back in regular contact with my family. He was severely frostbitten on both feet during harsh winter conditions in December 2010.

Mr. Rigney's Sallie Mae Teaching Award on display in Rigney Marcela's home.

Learning of Mr. Rigney's Frostbite

I will always wonder if things would have been different if I had followed my historic protocol and visited Mr. Rigney before going to my family Christmas party in Mount Airy, North Carolina, on December 18, 2010. Would we have even been able to find him in his deep mountain habitat? If so, would he have told us that his feet were causing him miserable pain? If he told us, would he have agreed to let us take him to the hospital?

I will never know the true answers to these questions, but one thing is sure: I wish we had not let the threat of snow deter us from going to his home located in the Blue Ridge Mountains on that cold, cold day. Perhaps we could have convinced him to seek medical attention for his frostbitten feet at that time and prevented the amputations that were to come on February 23, 2011.

It is truly an act of God that allowed me to find out about his hospitalization and diagnosed frostbite. My oldest son, Braxton, and I drove to Fancy Gap, Virginia, on December 29, 2010, to deliver a late Christmas gift to him only to find the Blue Ridge Parkway closed because of snowy weather. Knowing that there was no other way of getting to his home, I decided to go to the small clothing shop where his niece worked, leave the gift, and inquire about his health. Given that I didn't know his niece, I was doubtful that even these efforts would pay off, but I went anyway.

An older lady with blonde hair, makeup, and jewelry was working behind the counter. Knowing nothing of his niece's appearance, I asked her if a lady bearing the last name of "Rigney" still worked there.

She replied, "That is me. My name is Esther Mae Rigney."

I handed her the fruit basket and asked her if she would deliver it to Mr. Rigney since the snowy roads prevented me from giving it to him myself. I was shocked when she explained that it would be a few days before she would see him as he was being moved from Baptist Hospital in Winston-Salem, North Carolina, to Blue Ridge Nursing Home in Stuart, Virginia.

Knowing that this nursing home is located in the county where Mr. Rigney spent thirty-three years teaching in public schools, I knew he would likely be very happy there, but with confusion, I further inquired about the reasons for his hospitalization. Esther Mae explained that he was suffering extreme pain in his feet believed to be caused by poor circulation or frostbite. She told me that he would be arriving by ambulance at the nursing home at 4:00 PM that same afternoon. Given that it was already nearly 2:00 PM and I needed to get my son back home, I called Phyllis Eastridge, a mutual friend, and previous fellow teacher from Patrick County High School who lived in Stuart, and asked her if she could go to the nursing home and greet him so he would not be alone as he began the acclimation process.

My phone rang around 6:00 PM that same evening with Phyllis explaining that he did not arrive at the nursing home as planned. She further explained that the nursing home staff had no information indicating that he was coming at all. I hung up and called Mr. Rigney's favorite nephew, pleasantly nicknamed Junebug, and inquired about his current condition and the plans for admittance to the nursing home. He was uninformed about what would happen next as the social worker had indeed told him that the plan was to place him in the nursing facility. June bug encouraged me to call the Intensive Care Burn Unit at Bowman Gray Hospital in Winston-Salem, NC, where frostbite patients are treated and inquire of his condition myself.

I was fortunate enough to get a young nurse on the phone from the Intensive Care Burn Unit. He very professionally explained that he could not give me much information because of confidentiality guidelines, but he told me that Mr. Rigney was stable and his vital signs were good. He further confirmed that Mr. Rigney was indeed suffering tremendously from frostbite. I asked if there would be any amputations, but he said such information would need to come directly from the doctor.

He informed me that Mr. Rigney had been admitted to the hospital on December 21, 2010, and had received no visitors during that period, including Christmas Day. He further explained that he did not believe a nursing home was an immediate option at that time as he was physically unable to be moved. I gave the nurse my name and asked him if he would tell Mr. Rigney that I would be in to see him the next day.

True to my word, I arrived in Room 1010 of the Intensive Care Burn Unit at approximately 3:00 PM on December 30, 2010, to find Mr. Rigney looking disheveled and lonely with both feet bound in heavy white bandages. They had shaved his long beard leaving only a mustache, which was never part of his style.

I noticed the tiny dead poinsettia resting on the bed tray and hoped that it was not a symbol of what was to come. I also took note of the back issue of Rolling Stone and Consumer Report magazines—neither of which would have ever been of any interest to Mr. Rigney—and wondered how he had survived nine days with no contact with anyone outside the hospital walls. It surely appeared that his outlook was dismal, but upon seeing me,

Mr. Rigney sat up in bed and skipping the hellos, clearly commanded, "Get my pocketbook out of the drawer and hand it to me now."

I reached in the drawer to find a very thick wallet crammed with money and gave it to him as requested. He fumbled with it and took out three twenty-dollar bills, handed them to me, and said, "Go buy me some Red Man chewing tobacco right now." I asked if I should visit awhile and then go, and he responded, "No, go right now. You can visit when you get back."

I left the hospital returning about twenty minutes later, with all the tobacco that a local CVS pharmacy had in stock. Mr. Rigney stuffed his mouth full of tobacco and seemed to liven up tremendously. He said, "I knew you were my only hope. The nurse said you would be here today, and I knew you would get me some Red Man." I concluded my visit with him about two hours later with the promise that I would return the next day.

I did indeed return the next day and the next. We spent countless hours in Room 1010, reminiscing about our history as teachers in Patrick County, Virginia. I even took my laptop computer, so that we could electronically search for news of former co-workers. We talked about people whom I had not thought about in years. We enjoyed our time together, but the day of my return to school from Christmas break was quickly approaching, and it was painfully clear that Mr. Rigney was dreading it as much as I was.

He was becoming anxious as the doctors and nurses were once again speaking of the possibility of his placement in the nursing facility in Virginia. We tried to gather information from the social worker assigned to his case, but to no avail, as she refused to speak to me since I am not a relative. The forlorn look in Mr. Rigney's eyes alerted me to the fact that he needed me with him as a discussion of his hospital discharge to the care of a nursing home became more serious. I asked him if he needed me to take off work on Monday, January 3, 2011, so I could speak with his doctor. He reluctantly responded with a simple "yes," but I knew he hated the idea of my missing a day of school.

The nurses informed us that the doctors would be by around 10:00 AM on January 3, and at that time, they would enlighten us about his current condition and future medical plans. I arrived at the hospital before 9:00 AM to make sure I did not miss the doctors' visit.

When they arrived, Mr. Rigney asked me to wait outside, as he did not want me to see the condition of his feet when the doctors unwrapped them. While waiting, one of the doctors accidentally opened the door briefly revealing his unwrapped feet to me. At that particular moment, I was grateful that he didn't want me to see them, as the grotesqueness was far beyond anything I had ever imagined. They were completely black with splotches of red rawness, causing them to appear as though they had been damaged in a deadly fire. At that moment, I was skeptical as to whether he would ever recover, for I could not imagine the damage and pain such an invasive infection could create.

Once his feet were treated and re-wrapped, I entered the room, and the lead doctor informed me that his condition was stable. Explaining that I was aware of confidentiality rules, I asked if there was anything further he could tell me. He asked me to step into the hallway with the entire team of doctors, residents, and interns that were assigned to the case.

I was rather surprised when the lead doctor asked how long Mr. Rigney had been homeless. I responded that after his house burned in April 2010, he had been living in a small house located behind his nephew's home in the mountains and had never been homeless.

One of the interns insisted that he had been living in a "tent-city," but I assured them that he did not live in a tent, nor was he homeless. The intern ignored what I was trying to tell them, so I adamantly explained that after forty-nine years of teaching in public schools, he had retreated to his mountain home and lived primitively.

This false information about his homelessness had indeed been put in the medical report, as I saw it myself when hospital personnel gave me a copy to deliver to the nursing home. I suppose that is the reason the rumor followed him, and various people questioned me about it. This information was unequivocally false as he never lived in a tent.

Consequently, their next inquiry regarded how he came to be frostbitten. Not knowing, I tried to explain to them that when he was not teaching, he always lived like a hermit in the mountains and cut timber regardless of the severity of the weather conditions. I naturally assumed that Mr. Rigney had misjudged the record breaking cold December weather and stayed outside in intolerable conditions.

I would later learn from him that it was extreme cold, coupled with wetness that had caused the frostbite. He had relied too heavily on his waterproof boots to protect his feet.

Once we concluded our attempt at figuring out how the frostbite occurred, I was relieved to learn that since no family members had contacted them, the doctors were ready to talk to me about his condition and his future.

The lead doctor began by explaining the "frostbite in January; amputation in July" philosophy. I asked them if there was a possibility that he could make a full recovery without amputations, but they could not give me a definitive answer until the body had completed the natural healing process. They told me that they were fairly certain that he would be able to keep most of his right foot, but their professional prediction was the loss of his left foot. At any rate, surgery would likely be performed in July, and only time, motivation, and natural healing could tell the outcome.

Dr. Holmes, his surgeon, said that since Mr. Rigney's condition was stable, placement in a nursing home was appropriate at the time. I suggested the possibility of bringing him to my home, but the doctors were unsure if I could maintain a full-time teaching job and handle the acute care necessary for optimum healing.

Dr. Holmes suggested that to expedite my return to work, we should plan for the nursing home transfer the following day. After the doctors discussed nursing home placement with Mr. Rigney, the social worker, who still refused to talk to me, coordinated plans to transfer him the following morning. We were told that his condition was stable enough that I could take him in the car as opposed to sending him alone in an ambulance once his nephew, who held his Power of Attorney, gave permission.

Junebug was very appreciative of my visits to Mr. Rigney in the mountains, and at the hospital, so I knew he would have no problem granting permission to the social worker to release Mr. Rigney to me. The big problem was getting Junebug on the phone as he was hard to reach.

The day before his release, the nurses had tried relentlessly to reach him, but to no avail. Finally, about 4:00 PM that afternoon, we were able to get his wife, Esther Mae, on the phone. She explained that Junebug was in the mountains cutting timber. She offered to get him and bring him back to the house so that he could return our call. When he called back, he had to inform the social worker that I had his permission to transport Mr. Rigney to the nursing home.

The social worker asked, "Do you give permission to release George Rigney to Marsha Marcela, who will transport him to the nursing home?"

Junebug's response was, "Let her do whatever the hell she wants. They've been friends for over thirty years."

I arrived to take Mr. Rigney to the nursing home in Virginia on January 4, 2011, at approximately 10:00 AM. While he was ready to go, he was very anxious about his adjustment to such a confined situation. He even suggested that he would rather stay in the hospital, but that was not an option. Through his continuous, nervous chatter, he finally declared that "we will give the nursing home one week."

I asked him what he expected me to do after one week if he didn't like it. He didn't have a clear solution, but he said we would look at other options. I am still not sure what those "other options" were, but thankfully, he quickly adjusted to the nursing home.

The drive to the nursing home was quite tense as we were both very scared of the immediate future. We tried to talk about unrelated subjects, but somehow the conversation always made its way back to the real purpose of the trip. As we approached Patrick County, the beautiful Blue Ridge Mountains came into view. There was still a hint of glittering white snow adorning their tops. Those mountains meant so much to both Mr. Rigney and me, as that is where our friendship began. It seems ironic how such natural beauty can exist in both the most exhilarating moments of our lives as well as the lowest moments, such as this one.

Driving up the hill to the large white brick building that housed so many elderly, terminally ill patients, Mr. Rigney said, "Well, it doesn't look like much, does it?"

I found this statement rather ironic given the primitive conditions to which he was accustomed. He repeated his previous statement that "we will give it one week."

I stopped the car and went inside to inform the receptionist that George Rigney had arrived and needed to be admitted as a resident. By the time the words were out of my mouth, a parade of health care workers behind a single wheelchair came into my view. They were Mr. Rigney's former students, likely ranging in age from thirty to fifty, eagerly anticipating his arrival. When they greeted him at the car, a huge smile crept across his face, and he yelled, "How ya doin'?"

As he was being transported into the facility, he was explaining to me how he had taught all of those people who were bringing him inside. One of the ladies separated herself from the crowd and told him she was going to another part of the facility to get Ruth, his sister, who was also a resident. It appeared that after twelve years of seclusion in the mountains, Mr. Rigney was now surrounded by people who knew and loved him.

By the time I left him, a line of about twenty people had formed outside his door. I knew, yet continued to pray, that he would be all right. I also knew that despite time and distance, our friendship had never faltered, and we were going to be spending much time together throughout the process of his recovery.

As I drove home, I continued to reflect on the "what if" questions I had previously pondered. Even though I shall never know what might have happened had I visited Mr. Rigney on December 18, 2010, one thing that I did know is that his future was going to be filled with people who loved him—one of them being me.

My family and I visited Mr. Rigney every other weekend as long as he stayed in the nursing home.

Blue Ridge Nursing Center

By Betty Conner

George Rigney

One of Patrick County's most beloved teachers, George Rigney, is our resident of the month.

Rigney was born in Carroll County on June 7, 1932, the third of six children born to Robert and Mary Jane Meredith Rigney. He attended elementary school in Cana at a one-room school called Flint Hill. He then took classes through the American Correspondence School in Chicago. After successfully passing the Virginia High School Completion Examination, he received a graduation diploma from the State Board of Education in 1949.

Rigney began his teaching career in 1949 at Blue Ridge School, a one-room school beside the Blue Ridge Parkway in Carroll County. He taught there one year before the school was consolidated with another school. He then taught at several area schools including: Turner, Dewey, Round Knob, Elksboro, Pilot View, and St. Paul before going to Flat Rock School in neighboring North Carolina where he taught fifth grade English for five years.

He then came to Patrick County where he remained until his retirement in 1999. He taught at Stuart High School for three years and moved to Patrick County High when it opened in the fall of 1970.

When he began teaching, a bachelor's degree was not a requirement, but that changed and everyone had to be accredited. For ten years, he taught during the school year and attended Radford College in the summers to obtain his bachelor's degree. He con-

George Rigney

tinued for attend "summer school" another three years to achieve his master's degree. When asked what he did for fun, Rigney just smiled and said, "went to school."

He said that after retiring, he turned into a hermit, letting his hair and beard grow long. He helped his nephew cut and sell firewood and took care of their animals.

Rigney has dedicated his entire life to learning and teaching and as many residents of Patrick County know, his classes were always interesting and informative. He stated that each student is capable of learning, but each is different and you have to teach on their level.

He is a unique individual with a positive attitude that has served him well throughout his life. Although he never married nor had children of his own, he has set an example and helped in guiding thousands of our youth into adulthood. To name half of his accomplishments we would need to write a book—that might be an idea for his retirement—how about *George Rigney's Memoirs*? Now that would be an interesting read!

In 1973, Rigney was voted "Teacher of the Year" at PCHS and his distinctive voice was heard for 20

years calling out the students' names as they received their diplomas at graduation.

He left his home in Cana around 5 a.m., drove 50 miles to Patrick County to teach and often stayed after school to sponsor student activities. He is quick to let you know that he doesn't agree with a lot of the state mandates that teachers have to put up with today, with too much emphasis on paperwork and not enough on the students.

He came to reside with us here at Blue Ridge Nursing Center in January of this year. Each time you go by his room, you'll see him reading or talking with his many visitors. Many fellow teachers and students have made their way to visit and he loves to have company. Many thanks to Mr. Rigney (I can't bring myself to call him George) for sharing his story with others. Be sure to stop by for a visit!

Connor Knowles celebrated his second birthday on February 20. He celebrated with a party joined by family and friends at his home in Floyd. Connor is the son of Brian and Shannon Knowles, originally of Meadows of Dan. He is the grandson of Carlton and Barbara Largen of Meadows of Dan, Libby and Elmo Dalton of Meadows of Dan, Cathy Knowles of Stuart and Richard Knowles of Meadows of Dan.

Junebug

William Curtis Rigney, known to Mr. Rigney as Junebug, was his favorite nephew.

It would have been hard to be a friend to Mr. Rigney without meeting his favorite nephew, Junior, whom he affectionately called "Junebug." I thought everybody called him Junebug, but I would learn many years later that only Mr. Rigney called him that. Well, except for me, and I called him "Junebug" because...well, I thought everyone did.

Junebug was the son of Mr. Rigney's sister, Ruth. He was a very enterprising worker in the mountains and was known for clearing much of the timber that had once covered the properties now occupied by high-end summer homes. Mr. Rigney had been very involved in Junebug's work, and they were about as close as most fathers and sons.

Junebug also held Mr. Rigney's Power of Attorney, which forced him to make the hard decisions that came with that role. He would be the person I called to make arrangements to transport Mr. Rigney from the nursing home to his necessary doctor appointments. He and I also spoke frequently on the phone about Mr. Rigney's progress.

Junebug and his wife, Esther Mae, visited Mr. Rigney regularly while he was in the nursing home, and then visited him daily when he was released to live independently in an apartment. Their bond strengthened as Junebug sat with him for hours watching WWE wrestling and Virginia Tech football.

It was surely a blow in the spring of 2014 when Junebug started experiencing some serious stomach issues. He told me about them in a phone conversation and further explained that the doctors were treating him, but they weren't sure exactly what the problem could be. Of course, a series of numerous tests ensued, resulting in a very advanced case of pancreatic cancer.

Upon learning of Junebug's diagnosis, Mr. Rigney was in denial for quite some time. He kept thinking he would get well. At first, I believe that Junebug tried as hard as he could to downplay the seriousness of his condition to spare Mr. Rigney the worry of what would eventually happen. That became more and more difficult as Junebug's hospital stays became more frequent and lengthier over the next few months.

When Junebug returned home from one of his last hospital stays, I drove Mr. Rigney to Junebug's home in Fancy Gap so that they could spend some time together. We were able to get Junebug seated in a chair outside the car, where the two of them talked for a long time. I don't know the nature of their conversation because I sat on the porch with Esther Mae, so they could discuss whatever they wished. This would be the last time I ever took him to visit Junebug.

I attended Junebug's funeral and offered to take Mr. Rigney with me. He was never one to attend funerals, nor did he have the emotional fortitude. My husband stayed with him at the apartment while I went. The chapel at the funeral home was full of friends and family. When the officiating minister asked if anyone would like to speak of their experiences with Junebug, I felt compelled to say a few words on Mr. Rigney's behalf.

I told the congregation about the many lengthy phone conversations Junebug and I had as we tried to make Mr. Rigney comfortable after the amputations. I also mentioned the many phone calls Junebug had made to the hospital and nursing home, permitting me to transport Mr. Rigney. He was so good and cooperative, and I will be forever grateful for his acceptance of my family's relationship with Mr. Rigney.

I left the funeral home immediately following the service as I wanted to get back to Mr. Rigney's apartment before the procession left the funeral home. I knew that the hearse carrying Junebug's body would be passing directly in front of the window where Mr. Rigney sat, and I wasn't sure how he would react.

As expected, the procession passed as Mr. Rigney stared out the window. He said, "He was surely a good 'un, and he will be missed."

He died on July 3, 2014, at the age of 61 years. It would be less than twenty-four hours later that Junebug's mother, Ruth, Mr. Rigney's sister, would die. She had lived at the same nursing home at the same time as Mr. Rigney. When he was released from the nursing home, he saw her for the last time.

I would also learn the following week that his sister, Maggie, had passed away. These three deaths had followed the death of another nephew, Carlos, in June 2014. Mr. Rigney was overwrought with grief.

I went to visit Mr. Rigney about a week after Junebug's and Ruth's funerals. He was beside himself with grief and refused to leave his room.

He said, "I can't face people just yet."

Brenda Kaye, another niece, happened to stop by, so she and I encouraged him to leave his room even if it was just for a ride on the Blue Ridge Parkway. She finally said, "George, you've sat here long enough. Get off your ass and go somewhere." He stood up and started walking out the door.

I asked him where he would like to go.

He said, "Let's go to Dollar Tree. You can buy yourself something, and I can practice my walking."

When I asked him if he was sure he wanted to go out in public, he said, "Going to a store is all right. I just don't want to face people I know who might ask about Junebug's death."

We had a lovely day together, but Mr. Rigney's grief for Junebug lingered until his death about four years later.

Rigney Marcela's school portrait during his first year of teaching at
J.V. Washam Elementary School.

Rigney Marcela, nine months old, with Timber, the stuffed
wolf Mr. Rigney gave him for his first Christmas.
Timber continues to live with Rigney.

Marshall Rigney Marcela

Note: My son was named after George Rigney, so they developed a significant relationship, especially during the years of Mr. Rigney's recovery. This chapter is written by Rigney. It is only fitting that it be included in my story.

My name is Marshall Rigney Marcela. I take great pride in my name because each name is representative of one of the people that helped mold me into the person I am today. The last name is pretty self-explanatory. It comes from my dad, Dr. Mike Marcela. He has a doctorate in Special Education Administration and has served as an advocate for those who can't advocate for themselves for as long as I can remember.

My first name Marshall, which is a little bit harder to decipher, comes from my mother's first name, Marshalene. She has been a special education teacher since before I was born and has always gone above and beyond what I have ever seen any other teacher do for their students.

My middle name is what I go by, what is often mispronounced or just ignored because "Ricky" is easier, but to me the real reason and person behind that name means the world to me. I am named after a

Virginia teaching legend, Mr. George Daniel Rigney. He is whom I refer to as my grandpa. He is where this story begins.

To me, as a young child, Mr. Rigney was more of a legend than a person. Raised in a house of educators, his stories as a teacher were told to me like old mountain folk tales or some crazy legend like that of Bigfoot. I remember things like meeting him at the grocery store to buy dog food and him knowing every single person in the store. I remember seeing him pop out of the woods emerging from a small dirt road with a wolf, which lived with him. Sometimes he had a beard almost down to his belly button. I heard stories of him waking up at 5 AM to put chains on his tires so he could navigate the Blue Ridge Parkway to get to school on time. Things like that are unheard of, and when you do hear them, they kind of sound like when an old person says, "I used to walk uphill in the snow to school, both ways!" The only difference is Mr. Rigney did it.

During my younger years, I knew I was named after a "family friend" but did not understand the weight that carried or what Mr. Rigney would mean to me by the time he left this earth.

Just to give you some background as to why I have always associated the word "legend" with Mr. Rigney is because you could be anywhere in North Carolina and Virginia (and honestly it wouldn't surprise me if you just applied this to the whole world) and if there were more than ten people there, one of them would know Mr. Rigney.

I spent the bulk of my childhood in Huntersville, North Carolina, about an hour and a half minimum drive from Mr. Rigney. One Sunday, when I was eighteen years old, I gave the youth Sunday sermon at my church. With roughly one hundred people in attendance, I did not think the name of Mr. Rigney would mean much to people, so I used his actions to tell the story of how we can live a Christ-led life in the difficult times of today. Lo and behold, after church, an elderly woman walked up and asked if I had a copy of my sermon notes. She had sat too far away and couldn't hear very well, but she had heard the name Mr. Rigney and wanted to know if he was a teacher from Virginia. She had been quite fond of him.

I don't remember how she knew him or her name, but I could not believe in a different town with totally different demographics, there was someone who had crossed paths with Mr. Rigney.

If you've got good parents when you are a kid they are always having you do things because "it's what's best for you" or "you will understand why this is so important one day" and usually those words are followed by a request to do something that you probably weren't planning on doing.

Those words started coming around often when I was about sixteen years old. It is typically something like "Do your summer reading project" or "Get in bed early tonight," and I think everyone at some point has that old person in the family who needs to be visited regularly. The specific question for me was, "Can you go visit Mr. Rigney with me?" Now, almost a decade later, I know it is when your parents say, "You will thank me one day for making you do this," it is probably true and in my case, way more true than I ever thought it could be.

In December of my junior year of high school, the mountain man, Teacher of the Nation, Virginia native, Mr. Rigney had found himself in the hospital at the age of seventy-eight with frostbite on both of his feet-- so severe that he was placed in the intensive care burn unit.

Since he had never married and had no children, he had been in the hospital for over a week with no visitors. Also, not fully understanding the impact that Mr. Rigney had already imprinted on my mom's life, I was rather surprised to see her rapidly shift all her energy into making sure that he was okay. My mom spent the last few days of December running back and forth between Winston Salem, North Carolina, and Huntersville, where we were living at the time.

When I first started visiting Mr. Rigney in the hospital that year, I realized that I was finally going to get the chance to realize why I was named after this man. I had not seen him since I was a young boy, but his face lit up as he said, "That is MY boy." It caught me a little off guard at first, but with his never having children or grandchildren of his own, it made sense to me in a weird way. Also, I only remember having one living grandparent who lived in New Jersey, so I kind of liked the thought of having the old man consider me his grandchild. Plus, he seemed like an easy man to make happy, so it was a task I could handle. Also, at the time, I knew it made my mom happy during a tough time, so I was grateful to step in when I could.

We lived about one and a half hours away from Mr. Rigney when he was in the hospital and two hours once he was finally moved to a nursing home, so it was always an all day trip to see him. He and my mom truly were best friends; it was awesome to see. I have never seen two people hold a conversation for twelve hours so easily, even though Mr. Rigney did most of the talking. When we came, no matter how long we were there, he was going to tell us everything he planned on telling us.

My early visits with him were quite boring to be honest. I usually came in and updated Mr. Rigney on my life, found a Sudoku puzzle, and eventually took a nap on his bed. He would never sit on his bed when we came to visit; he always made his way into his wheelchair. At first, I thought my nap might have bothered him and my mom, but they would talk for hours about people who died before I was even born, and it was just tough to stay awake. As the number of these visits piled up, I realized he actually liked them and looked forward to them.

He would select the puzzles out of the newspapers for me, so I didn't have to look for them. He would locate the nicest pen he could find, and when he was capable, he would make sure his bed was cleared off with a blanket on it for me. During this phase in our relationship, it wasn't uncommon for him to refer to me as "Sleeping Beauty." Even though, every time he got a new nurse or caretaker, he would insist I introduce myself to them as his boy. It often went like this:

Me: Hello, you must be the new nurse. I just wanted to introduce myself! I am Rigney, Mr. Rigney's boy!

Nurse: Oh! I didn't know he had a grandson.

Me: Oh, he doesn't. I am not his grandson or son, just his boy

Nurse: (Looking at me strangely) Okay then....

It was always awkward and uncomfortable, but I know it made him happy especially if he could hear me refer to me as his boy. I got over the awkwardness of my encounters, and my mom and I always got a kick out of them because she got the same treatment. He would do the same thing with her, as my mom was always Mr. Rigney's "unofficial daughter," and people never totally understood how we fit into the equation. I am not sure my mom and I did either, but we did know he loved us and we loved him.

Our visits, during which I took my naps, at first included the whole family, but they did not stay like that forever. After a few months or so of recovering in the nursing home, the decision was made that Mr. Rigney was going to have to become a double amputee. He would be forced to lose the bottom half of his right leg and half of his left foot.

Knowing this would be a life altering decision, I figured things would change or potentially end. From Mr. Rigney's perspective, at least in front of me, it was just time to shift into another chapter of life. He never showed any fear or anxiety in front of his boy; he didn't want me to be scared or worried for him. Watching an eighty-year-old man tackle a double amputation like it was just another road bump in life was truly inspiring.

Over the next several months, all our visits were still in the nursing home, but the mood started to shift a little bit. Mr. Rigney was no longer this old man stuck due to an injury; he was motivated to do whatever it took to get back on his feet. I remember him telling me he hoped to get his driver's license back eventually. Knowing he was a man with no feet and horrible hearing, I knew this wasn't exactly a possibility, but he declared that nothing was going to stop him from living his best life.

During the months of constant appointments and treatments, I did not go and see Mr. Rigney as much as my parents did. He never really wanted me to see and notice him during the worst times, but my parents drove him anywhere he needed to go, so they always filled me in on the details. Plus, I was sixteen or seventeen years old and not stupid, so there wasn't much I did not know.

His progress was remarkable, and honestly, another turning point in our relationship. This was right around the time that I was getting independent enough to visit him on my own. He would never say it, but I am pretty sure my mom was without a doubt his best friend, and I was his favorite visitor. When I visited him by myself, naps slowly started to stop as funny stories and memories started to form.

I loved a good story about Mr. Rigney raising hell or letting someone know his true feelings. He was one of the nicest people ever, but he did not respond well to some healthcare workers, bless their hearts, and any unknown visitors that he felt were wasting his time. And by far his least favorite was someone you could just tell right off the bat was not a good person. We could sit and laugh and cut up for hours. But what was amazing was that even with no legs, our visits weren't just the two of us sitting in a room.

My favorite memories of Mr. Rigney in the nursing home are when he would have to practice walking. It was slow, initially with a walker and even more so with the cane. It really wouldn't have been that bad if Mr. Rigney did not have to stop walking to talk. He talked all the time on hiswalks. So, they very gradually started to feel reminiscent of stop and go traffic that never fully went.

He always encouraged me to do whatever I needed to have fun. Our go-to was the good ole' reverse race. That's when I would take the wheelchair, and he would walk. It was a true turtle and hare situation. But he got the biggest smile out of seeing me almost fall out of the chair popping wheelies and doing 360's. Since I never was injured as a kid, I never had any wheelchair experience. We did have a better time taking a stroll down a dilapidated nursing home hallway than anyone else in the world could have.

Things started to feel stable as far as Mr. Rigney's life went. He was in the nursing home awhile, and although he did not like it, I thought it was where he was meant to spend out his days. I mean, he never had lived with the accommodations that a typical person would need, so it seemed like a forced step up. Mr. Rigney did not get forced to live the way he did not want to. I got a call one day from Mom, who was on her way to Hillsville, Virginia. I remember her telling me, "Mr. Rigney escaped the nursing home!"

As she filled me in on the details, it sounded like he decided to go, arranged a ride, wheeled himself outside, and left. I don't know if that is what I would describe as an escape, but for a man with no legs, I think it's as close as you can get. He had, with the help of his nephew, found refuge in what I describe as an abandoned hotel. It wasn't though. I realized quickly it was a resting point for some strange souls that passed through Hillsville.

Mr. Rigney had found his home. One bedroom, with something like a bathroom, a recliner, a spot for his wheelchair, and various other foldable seats for his visitors. And I don't know this for sure, but at the age of eighty in 2012, I believe he got his first mini-fridge and television. This was the step-up that Mr. Rigney thought was ideal.

Once he was settled in The Blue Ridge Motel or whatever name had been given to that place, my visits were primarily made on my own. My mom can't sit still; even as she gets older, she always has to be going to see someone or doing something. I could tell that she was getting tired of driving back and forth from Charlotte to Virginia. Not because she did not want to see Mr. Rigney--she would have driven to see him every day if she could have, but traffic crossing the lake leaving Charlotte was enough to make you scream.

We decided to split up our visits. I could go one weekend a month; she would go two, and then that left only one weekend for someone else to pick up the slack. Or we would just go again. Neither of us ever wanted him to get lonely. We also never went during the week because he would not allow us to miss school.

At the time, I was finishing up high school, and my parents were working in the school system and always had to be there. Mr. Rigney wholeheartedly believed we needed to be at school every day, giving it our all because Mom's students and my education were more important than visiting him.

I loved going to visit Mr. Rigney. We settled into the best routine. I would arrive at his apartment, and he would shake my hand and give me a Sudoku puzzle. I loved doing puzzles because I could zone out and let him ramble about people whom I was not alive to know and had never heard of, and he loved making fun of me when I couldn't do the puzzles. He used to say, "If you could ever complete one of those, I might hang it on the wall." No puzzle ever made it to the wall.

After the puzzle and about an hour later, he would ask me if I was hungry, and I would say, "Yes." We would walk to the car which round trip took about an hour, because like I mentioned earlier, he did not walk and talk at the same time, so he took a step about every two hundred words. We had to walk the length of the hotel to the handicap ramp so I could pull the car around, and he could get in. Other than putting his walker in the car, I never helped. I don't think he wanted me to offer, and he respected the fact that I gave him enough credit to do it on his own.

We would then get food at Burger King; I still think of Mr. Rigney when I eat Burger King, and I only still eat there because it brings back such good memories. After that, we would head down the mountain to a specific gas station where the attendant would pump the gas for us. He would hand the attendant $50 and tell him to keep the change, no matter how much gas I needed. He always looked out for anyone who was hardworking and kind. After that, we would head back toward his room, walk back down the sidewalk, and talk for another half hour.

He always liked to ask me when I walked in "Are you only here to visit or do you have awhile?" and I always knew what that meant: he was ready to go for a ride. And not just our normal routine. We would still get food and gas, but when we went on a ride, it was because he had something or someone he wanted to see. I never really cared to visit people, actually hated it, but I loved to drive, so I didn't care how long it took to get there or where it was. I usually had fun.

My mom got the worst of these rides; he would take her all sorts of places where he visited with a variety of people. He took her to the places he knew I wouldn't want to go. He knew Mom didn't want to go to some of them, but he knew she could never turn him down. Even though we dreaded some of them, I think Mom would agree the times spent in the car taking Mr. Rigney the places that made him happy was one of the absolute most fulfilling things you could do with your Saturday. And looking back, those are the times that I miss Mr. Rigney most. When you wanted to go for a drive, there was not another person more prepared to ride shotgun.

Some of our first rides were for him to teach me about his life. He told me a lot about his life as we wrapped through the Virginia mountains. When we would pull up to the house of a friend or relative or an old school, there was that brief moment of silence while all of the nostalgia rushed back to him before he could start telling whatever story was rooted in our current location. For me, that's what made these rides so special.

Our rides started off short. The first couple we visited lived off the Blue Ridge Parkway near where he had lived with his wolf, Brownie. By the time Mr. Rigney passed, I could've driven to his old house with my eyes closed. It was the first right turn off the parkway onto Elk Spur Road, and then you would follow that all the way up the mountain, past the point that my mom would always say, "Look boys, this is where we drive off the edge of the earth." And it truly looked like it. You would get near the top, pass Junebug's house, and reach a cul de sac. At the end of a tiny, overgrown, dirt path, was where his house had been.

I never saw the house, but I walked down that road after he died and couldn't find a structure that fit the description of Mr. Rigney's living quarters. It did not sound like much, literally three or four walls and a door. It is okay that I never saw that place as Mr. Rigney painted the description he wanted me to have and that is all I needed.

Our visits quickly went from taking drives up to his old road to taking trips up to his old neighbors' homes. Wake Forest University owned his neighboring land. The university had two retreat houses tucked up in the hills on the Blue Ridge Parkway, and their driveway was right next to Mr. Rigney's road. The houses were huge and hard to get to. For some people, the houses would have been considered dream mountain vacation homes. I thought it was crazy that million dollar homes would share the end of the road with Mr. Rigney and his shack. We would pull up and drive right through the gate; it didn't matter if people were there or not. We would ignore the multiple "NO TRESPASSING" signs and find a place to park the car and look out at the view.

For a while, if anyone was there, they just asked what we were doing or asked us to leave. But eventually, they put up a fence that had to be unlocked just to enter their driveway. So, they must have noticed and minded more than we ever thought. But we didn't care; Mr. Rigney always did whatever he wanted.

The gate to enter the Wake Forest land was right next to the Rigney family cemetery, where Mr. Rigney was laid to rest, so whenever I visit his grave, I am reminded that beauty can come from anywhere whether it be beautiful mansions with all the bells and whistles or Mr.

Rigney's little shanty down that tiny, overgrown, little dirt road where you can find beauty and appreciate the nature around you.

To this day, Mr. Rigney's love for animals is something that was easily transferred to me. We always grew up with animals in my house. The typical count was four indoor cats and two outside dogs. It just seemed standard to me, but Mr. Rigney had a different standard for choosing his pets. He had a friend that as a gift connected him with a wolf breeder somewhere in Virginia and drove him out to pick out a "wolf-dog" as Mr. Rigney called it.

That wolf was a bigger part of my childhood than most people know. Mr. Rigney gave me a stuffed wolf upon my entrance to this world, and Timber has a special place in my house even though I am 26 years old. Timber inspired me to love wolves.

As a child, I collected anything that had a wolf on it. I still have a statue that I got on a family vacation to Myrtle Beach. I spent all of my spending money on it. Even though my Dad told me multiple times to carry it, I tried to slip it onto the luggage cart. I did and it immediately tumbled off the top, fell, and broke into many pieces. My dad was mad, but just like any great father, once we got home, he went to work gluing it back together.

As I got older, I took it one step further. I got my own big dog. His name is Howie and he is a black lab/chow mix. He is everything most people hate in a dog. He is stubborn, can be mean looking (although I think he's beautiful), has a mean bark, and weighs right around 100 pounds. He is not a dog for the non-dog person. I love him like a firstborn son, and he loves me like I am the only person on the planet worthy enough for him. The relationship with my dog might seem insignificant to some, but I know that is how Mr. Rigney was with Brownie, and that makes it incredibly special to me.

Brownie passed away before Mr. Rigney had to worry about his feet or where he was going to live, but in the meantime, Mr. Rigney had a fox. The fox's name was Fox. He told me by that point he figured it would outlive him, so why bother giving it a name. He said the fox was awesome, but it just wanted to sit there and be rubbed all the time. He said it was just like having a house cat, but he didn't want a housecat. Most people would have thought he didn't like that fox, but based on the fact that he took care of it for years and spoke of it almost as much as he did Brownie showed me he cared for that little thing. It didn't matter what it was; if it was living and breathing and needed care, Mr. Rigney would be there for it.

Once Mr. Rigney knew I was capable of driving him anywhere he needed to go, he started switching the locations on me regularly. My least favorite trips were the visits to people's homes. I did not enjoy them for several reasons. The first reason being, I did not know where any of the places were, and he did not know any of the addresses. So, I had to trust the directions of an eighty-plus year old man. And sometimes these trips would be up to an hour away, so I had to learn to trust Mr. Rigney.

The next reason I did not like these particular visits were I did not know any of these people, and without his legs, Mr. Rigney couldn't go to the door. I would have to ring the doorbell and explain who I was and why I was there. They would come out to the car and visit with Mr. Rigney.

Once again, my entrance went like this:

Me: Hello, my name is Rigney. I am here with Mr. Rigney

Visitor: WHO???

Me: I am Rigney, and I am here with George Rigney. He wants to visit you.

Visitor: OHHHH! Where is George? I can't wait to see him. Take me to him. It's been years. You're Rigney? Wow, are you his grandson?

Visitor: Nope, I am just Rigney, just follow me to the car, and he is there waiting for you!

And they would continue to talk and catch up, rarely taking less than a half-hour. I typically tried something to keep myself busy. If they had dogs, I always invited to dogs into the air-conditioned car to sit and keep me company while Mr. Rigney visited. I gave every dog I encountered a new name, but his barber owned my favorite dogs to visit.

He and his barber, Andy, were about the same age, and you would have thought they were best friends. They knew each other well and had many mutual friends. They enjoyed talking to each other and catching up on old times. I enjoyed watching the two of them together, and I entertained his dog. Andy loved my bright red Dodge Charger. This was my favorite place to take Mr. Rigney.

Another fond memory I have was visiting with some couple that Mr. Rigney had been friends longer than I was alive. The first time I took him there, an old man wearing no shirt answered the door and did not seem to enjoy the fact that I was there. But that all changed once I was able to explain that I had his friend George in the front seat, and he wanted to visit. Shortly after, the man, still with no shirt on, emerged with his wife. They visited for about an hour as I sat at a table in their yard and tried to sleep with my eyes open.

About halfway through their visit, the man, still with no shirt on, came over and sat with me. He had two puzzles or optical illusions with him. He kept making this lever look like it was stuck and another rope that looked impossibly tied around a ring. He told me that at some point everything seemed difficult, unknown, and impossible, but if you find someone to show you the way, all your questions would be answered. He made the connection that Mr. Rigney was that person for many, many people. He let me keep the two little puzzles. He finished up his visit, and Mr. Rigney and I made our way down their deathtrap of a driveway.

This story will always stick with me because it put one of the most complex people I had ever met into one simple thought. Mr. Rigney was here to guide people through life. To be that person, you look back on knowing that he made an impact even though he didn't have too. It is people like this that open up worlds of opportunities for you, just by being.

My least favorite visit ever might have just been the most eventful. For starters, Mr. Rigney always chewed tobacco. He told me the keys to living long were never to get married and to chew tobacco. Both pieces of advice I ignored, but he told me to ignore them, so it was okay. We were driving somewhere, and I looked over, and Mr. Rigney had thought the window was down. So, he turned and spit directly into the window. It was disgusting. Like I wanted to throw up. Very slowly, I saw him look at me and then discreetly try and lift his rag to wipe it off. The only problem was, he just smeared it and made it even worse. I knew he felt bad because he didn't say anything and just kept trying to clean it. I ignored it altogether and kept things moving.

Funny enough, when I told my mom later what had happened, she laughed because the same thing had happened when he was with her too. Anyway, we were on the way to see "the drunk preacher." That is all I knew because that is how Mr. Rigney referred to her. I asked why and he said because she got drunk and walked down the road butt naked in the middle of the night. Why were we going to see this person??? I didn't know, but I laughed at his story because just imagining it was crazy enough.

We arrived at a broken down home with overgrown grass and junk lying everywhere. Mr. Rigney told me to ring the doorbell and tell them who we were. I got out of the car, made it about twenty feet, and a raccoon ran across the year. Being the city slicker I am, I ran for cover and jumped in the car. I told Mr. Rigney nobody was home, and we would have to try again later.

Another x-factor in our visits was the strange looks we got as I drove my bright red Dodge Charger with tinted windows, black rims, and no muffler through rural Virginia. As I was preparing to pull away from the drunk preacher's house, someone was knocking at my window. Terrified as I was, they had seen me attempt to come to ring the doorbell and wanted to know what I wanted. I explained I had Mr. Rigney, and all was well from there.

He visited with the young man, whom I believe was the drunk preacher's son. I never did get to meet the drunk preacher, but as we were driving away, Mr. Rigney said, "I am glad we got to see them, but they are crazy as hell." Even though I never got to see the drunk naked preacher, I was just left with the already disgusting, strange image I had conjured up in my head. The real lesson behind this visit had sunk in. Mr. Rigney checked in on them, not because he particularly liked them (even though he did more than most probably did), but because he felt compelled to check on the people that had been a part of his life no matter how or why. He took it upon himself to look out for people who might not have anyone else looking out for them.

The rides that I will forever cherish the most, and the place we went most often, was the alpaca farm. It sounds strange, but that place taught me some very important things about life. It was a small farm off the Blue Ridge Parkway, not far from where he used to live. We originally went because Mr. Rigney wanted the low-down on the owners. He read in the paper that they were Virginia locals who had always made their money farming alpacas. Mr. Rigney, for some reason, and I still don't know why was convinced that they were "immigrants from Florida."

He knew they were not what people would have typically referred to as immigrants, but to him, they were originally from Florida and moved to Virginia; therefore, they were immigrants. He couldn't understand why they would be lying. Regardless, that was reason enough for both of us to need to go and further investigate. Who doesn't like uncovering someone trying to profit off of claiming to be a mountain alpaca farmer when they are actually from Florida!

On the way over, I was positive Mr. Rigney had pointed us in the wrong direction, but I drove two hours before without question. We always ended up in the right place, so I figured he was right this time too. He was, and we pulled in a small parking lot with a decent sized, white barn with a souvenir shop attached. There was no way he could physically go in the gift shop, and we couldn't see the alpacas, which were our main interests in going.

So, Mr. Rigney told me to pull around and drive down this dirt access road that was covered with NO TRESPASSING signs. He told me to ignore the signs and assured me that "My boy is the best driver there ever was and could get out of anything so just keep driving," and so I did.

We drove until we were right up next to the alpacas. They were the young ones, so they were outgoing and crowded near the car to wonder at us, just as we were at them. Then Mr. Rigney rolled down the window, like a kid at the Lazy 5 Ranch, and started whistling and talking to them. He said things like "Come here, Boy, I want to take you home," "You look like you are the mean bitch of the bunch," "Why won't you come over here?" and "You see that cute one over there; he's got some fur!" That was one of my all-time favorite Mr. Rigney moments.

After we sat there for a while, like at least a half-hour, Mr. Rigney's moment came. The owner approached our car, and politely asked what we were doing. I explained that my grandpa (because in times like this, it was much easier than explaining our actual relationship) had no legs and couldn't get out to walk. Before I could finish, Mr. Rigney chimed in, "It doesn't matter what the sign says, my boy is the best driver there is, and he can get us out of here, no problem, so don't even worry about us." I think the guy got the vibe that we were staying to look at the alpacas and would be back again multiple times to do the same thing.

He stuck around and talked for a little while, which might have been a mistake because Mr. Rigney immediately asked, "Where are ya from?" He responded with the name of some small rural area in Virginia that sounded familiar. Mr. Rigney then followed up, "No, what part of Florida?" The man seemed confused and responded that he had never lived in Florida. Mr. Rigney then explained how no one with that last name had lived in that area of Virginia since he had been alive.

I appreciate the owner of that farm because he just brushed it off, told us to enjoy our time, and to be careful getting out. He was foreshadowing the difficulty I would have navigating my mom's Lincoln Town Car in between a tractor, an industrial sized tiller, and a fence holding thirty alpacas. But regardless, I guess my skills lived up to the hype because I successfully got us out of there.

We visited the alpacas more times than I can remember, and every time he smiled and acted like a kid in a candy shop. He taught me several lessons by making that our usual visit spot. The main one being that you should enjoy the little things.

Life moved on. I was in college after living near Charlotte for more than a decade. Life for me was fast, doing everything I could in the shortest amount of time possible. Soaking in everything but moving through it so quickly that I was bound to miss things. The alpacas were a representation to me that you need to slow down and find joy in the things that you would usually drive right past. There is beauty in nature, and there is beauty in slowing down and appreciating the life you have around you and not seeking more life somewhere else. It was a symbol that everything you need can be encapsulated by a living, breathing being standing right there in front of you. Those alpacas made an 85-year-old feel like a child and made me open my eyes to the little things.

The other lesson I learned was: What is life if you don't do what you want to do? Ignore the NO TRESPASSING signs and enjoy life. Now and then risking a little trouble for a memory that would last a lifetime is worth it. It is a good thing Mr. Rigney was old when we met because if we were both young, we would've gotten in all sorts of troubles.

Our trips to the alpaca farm are one of the things that sticks with me the most. I have turned it into a life motto that I will always live by:

"Don't forget to stop and see the alpacas every once in a while." It sums up everything those trips meant to me and everything they meant to him.

Since he passed, I have not gone to the alpaca farm, and I probably never will again. It just couldn't be the same without him, but I will never stop living that way. I will always stop and enjoy the little things, and the present, and I will always dabble in a little trouble. It is the way he would want it.

The longest ride we ever had was probably the most important to Mr. Rigney. Around the time of this ride, I had begun college and was studying to join the family business. For most people, that actually revolves around some sort of business, but for our family, that was education. My dad worked his way up the educational ladder the way that I think everyone else wants too. He studied at Wake Forest for undergraduate, Appalachian State for his graduate degree, and finally, Virginia Tech to get his dual doctorate in Special Education and Public School Administration. He chose wonderful, well-respected universities, and used his knowledge to become one of the most respected educators to ever come through the school systems. I know because now I work in Charlotte-Mecklenburg schools, where he served the bulk of his career, and I can't say my last name anywhere without someone asking if I am Mike's son.

My mom is no slouch either on the teaching front. She is the one whom I got to see in action, and it was a sight to see. She obtained her undergraduate and graduate degrees from Appalachian State. It's only right that this is where my parents met, currently live, and plan to retire. They live in a beautiful log cabin that Mr. Rigney would have marveled at.

Mom took her teaching degrees and put them to use and is still, currently, to this day, doing the good work. I grew up watching her do things like buy her students groceries, drive them to basketball practice, supply their family Christmas, stand up for students who fell on the wrong side of the racial divide, and many more countless acts that you don't normally hear about a teacher doing. She is the best teacher I have ever gotten to witness.

Even though he didn't get the full teaching itch, my brother even took a job as an educational attorney when he first graduated law school. So, you could say teaching was in our blood. Mr. Rigney had nicknames for all my other family members: they were "The Doctor, who was my dad, "The Lawyer," who was my brother, and then Ms.

Honeycutt, which was my mom's maiden name. I would get my nickname once I completed college.

Since he knew I was going to be a teacher, and really everyone knew since I had vocally expressed that I wanted to be a teacher since birth, he wanted to take me to see all the places that he had taught in the past. He did not tell me this because he knew it was going to take a while, but I did get a history lesson this day, and the legend of Mr. Rigney became a walk through the personal life of the person sitting right next to me.

We started at a one-room schoolhouse, or what we thought had once been the building where he taught. He explained to me how, when he was eighteen years old, he took the high school state equivalency exam, passed, and began teaching. He taught a class with multiple grade levels. He would arrive early, fill the potbelly stove with wood to heat the place, and he would get to work. Mr. Rigney explained that his best teaching was done when it was done to each student's level. "Meet them where they are at, and take them where you want them to go" was the lesson he was trying to teach me in this spot. This was when I realized I was about to get a teaching lesson from the best, and I needed to soak it all in.

The second place was a church that had been used as a one-room schoolhouse. It was right down the road from the first one. He has similar stories here, but I did not get the same vibe from him that we had gotten in the first place. He used to say things like, "Find someone who understands you and wants you to do your best because then you can do your best. And if they don't want you there, you better not stay." So, I always assumed that Patrick County High School must have been the right fit for Mr. Rigney.

As we would drive around, Mr. Rigney would point out spots that were significant to him. One of my favorites was the side of the highway just a couple miles down the road from the Food Lion, where we used to try and find him. He told me about how one time he and Brownie, his wolf, were riding to Food Lion, and Brownie decided to run over Mr. Rigney's lap and jump out the window. Mr. Rigney promptly grabbed him by the leg. He then proceeded down the road as normal, except the wolf was still dangling out the side of the truck clinched by Mr. Rigney. As I was sitting there laughing at the image he had created, Mr. Rigney stoically turned and looked at me and said, "Brownie never tried that again," and then he began to chuckle. Like I said, looking back, I did take a trip to the past on this ride.

Our next stop was a long one; he wanted to show me where the great fire that burned down Meadows of Dan Elementary School. To my knowledge, he never taught at the school, but you could tell that he mourned the loss of a school and the toll that it could have on a community. It had happened a few years before, so there was already a new school built and no evidence of a massive fire.

When we were on the way to the Meadows of Dan, he told me about how he obtained his college degree. He was so proud to have a degree from the teaching program at Radford College, which at the time was intended for women. It was my understanding that he was the first man to get a degree from Radford teaching college. He obtained his degree in a very unusual way. He completed his courses over the span of ten years, attending classes only during the summer.

He couldn't attend college during the typical semesters because he was still actively teaching. I always thought it was hilarious that he was working to obtain his teaching degree while teaching. That wouldn't happen in today's world.

On top of this already unorthodox way, he hitchhiked many days to make it to class. He told me he would wake up "at the crack of dawn" and hike to the main road. From there, he would hitchhike to Radford if he couldn't meet his usual ride. The driver worked somewhere around Radford, but if Mr. Rigney rode with him, it required a ten mile round trip walk to meet him. At this time, his primary mode of transportation was still walking.

To me, that showed his dedication to being an educator and furthering his education. He saw education as a gift, and at no point should it be wasted. He also believed it was partly on the teacher if a student didn't value education. I had and still have never heard of someone going through the hurdles that Mr. Rigney had to get an education.

On this lengthy ride, I was grateful he didn't ask me to take him to Radford. He would never typically ask me to go somewhere that far away. He would drop hints to my mom about places he would like to visit, and she would plan trips for them. Looking back, it would have been cool to take him to Radford. He was very proud of his degrees, but a few years earlier, his home had burned with everything in it. So, with that, went his original degrees.

My mom, at some point, put a lot of time and energy into replacing those degrees. Once she did, they hung on his wall and were eventually moved into a family member's house after he died.

Mom also got him a Radford class ring. She bought it for him but insisted that I give it to him for Christmas. She said he would like it better if it came from me. So, I did, and it was his prize possession.

Mr. Rigney did not care much for possessions in general, but this was different. Every time anyone visited and had not seen it before, he said, "Look at what my boy got me. It's a class ring from Radford College." He loved it. It was so simple, just a simple silver ring, with the famous Radford clock tower, the year he graduated, and what I believe was a big ruby in the middle. I know that he died happier having that, and his being buried with it made things a little easier for my mom.

Even though we did a lot of driving around, we still have some crazy memories of things that happened without leaving his one-bedroom hotel room. He had some crazy neighbors that moved in throughout his tenure there. Some people were nice and forged relationships that Mr. Rigney spoke highly about all the time, and then some others did not get mentioned unless accompanied by a curse word.

Either way, if you took your time to visit Mr. Rigney or if we took the time to visit you, your picture was hanging on his wall. We called it his Wall of Fame. My family had its own wall. Mr. Rigney had his own section displaying his degrees, school pictures, his retirement letter from

President Clinton, the issue of *Newsweek* which featured an article that highlighted him as one of the nation's best teacher, and a laminated copy of his final evaluation on which he was marked exceptional in every single category. And the rest of the wall space was covered with everyone that Mr. Rigney wanted a picture with for at least seven years. He almost filled the entire thing. He loved to look at the people he visited.

There was a couple who lived a few doors down for a little while. I never knew their names, but they had a toddler named Liam, whom Mr. Rigney loved. It was interesting to me because I had never seen Mr. Rigney with small children, but he loved that kid. He talked about him nonstop for some time. I also found it interesting that he showed a ton of compassion towards Liam's dad. The dad was a struggling addict who, according to Mr. Rigney, was a wonderful father when he was sober, but like many, he had a temper and struggled to hold it together when he was using or drinking. Mr. Rigney would tell me how this man's disease made it so hard for him to reach his full potential.

He talked about his hopes that the family would leave the hotel, and the father would get sober and be the father that Liam needed. Mr. Rigney had faith in that dad, even though he had not given Mr. Rigney legitimate proof that he deserved it. But it didn't matter, Mr. Rigney saw a talented, smart young toddler and a dad with only the best intentions for his son.

This was the teacher in Mr. Rigney coming out. He believed in everybody unless they made it clear that they did not want Mr. Rigney's help. He was there to support anyone in any way that she could. Liam's family moved on, and we never saw them again, but Mr. Rigney still talked about the hopes and dreams he had for their family.

There was also this guy that lived next door to him for several years. He was a big guy who, I think, suffered from diabetes complications, and struggled to get around. Mr. Rigney would always ask me to knock on his door and say hello. Mr. Rigney hated the smell of the food that the man cooked in his room, and he wanted me to get a whiff of it. Mr. Rigney was also obsessed with his Kia Sol. He loved that little boxed shaped car. I don't know why, but he would've bought it if he could.

The neighbor that sticks with me the most is the "Barefoot Prophet." He was about 75 years old, 6 foot 5 inches tall, African American, and barefoot. He was extremely proud to have not worn shoes, at that time, for about twenty-seven years. He had been in the military, a truck driver, and now a self-proclaimed prophet who was told by God to give up his shoes so that he could learn through suffering what was truly valuable in life. He was one of the saddest, yet most intriguing, people I have ever met.

It was very evident that this man struggled with what seemed like a severe case of Post-Traumatic Stress Disorder from being in the Vietnam War. He would tell Mr. Rigney and me about vivid nightmares that kept him up all night long. He would hear noises and have constant visions of war terrors he must have gone through at a much younger age.

He also had a very complex and hypocritical belief system. For example, he was adamant that we should line up members of the LBGTQ community and execute them. He would then speak of the mass amount of rights that all citizens should have access to regardless of race, color, gender, or sexuality. He didn't believe in violence but thought the mass genocide of certain cultural groups was necessary.

There was once a newspaper article printed about him, and he wrote several messages on it. It was unlike anything I had ever seen; you could see the frantic writing as if he were trying to get down as many words as he could to document all the different thoughts that were pouring from his mind. Memories from the war, hate speech on politicians, Bible verses that looked like chicken scratch. There was no rhyme nor reason to what he wrote. Letters and words were written sideways, upside down, over other things, on the front, on the back. It was almost scary, but it made me realize that he was a person struggling from some difficult circumstances, doing what he could to make it through the days. He deserved to be treated like anyone else.

I saw this through Mr. Rigney, who would sit and cut up with the "prophet" for hours. Not that he soaked in anything the "prophet" said, but there were times when they both needed company and had each other. My favorite memories with the "prophet" were when Mr. Rigney would try to get a rise out of him by joking around and tell me that he and the "prophet" were going to get married. The "prophet' would immediately refute these claims and layout all the other options he was willing to explore before that would happen--the most common one being death. And Mr. Rigney laughed the whole time. You would never convince Mr. Rigney to think of someone differently because of their race, gender, or sexuality, but he sure would pick on you if you tried.

The "prophet" was a lost individual who completely wrote off his daughter for having a child out of wedlock. Even though she married her child's father and attempted to repair the relationship so that the "prophet" could have a relationship with his grandchild, he condemned her and her child to hell. I understood that the "prophet" did not understand the things he was saying, and he wanted to believe them. But once again, Mr. Rigney taught me that there is good in everyone.

Being a Christian, I always appreciated when the "prophet" prayed for me, which was every time he saw me. I often wonder if the "Barefoot Prophet" is still alive and still prophesying. He was one of the strangest, most eclectic humans I ever met, and he passed right through Mr. Rigney's old dilapidated hotel room.

I even brought some of my friends to visit Mr. Rigney. I brought my friend Cris, who is from Romania. Mr. Rigney was convinced he was Samoan even though we told him multiple times he wasn't. So, his nickname, naturally, was "The Samoan." My friend Nick came, and he was "the little boy" because Nick was a scrawny kid when Mr. Rigney met him. The last friend he met was Ethan, who was in school for being an engineer but hated math. So, Mr. Rigney called him "the mathematician." Mr. Rigney only met them a handful of times but asked about them every time I visited. In some way, he touched each of their lives.

As I mentioned earlier, Mr. Rigney told me the two keys to living long were chewing tobacco and never getting married. Even though he said never to get married, the girl he described as "the most beautiful woman I have ever seen," and my now-wife was a frequent visitor. He loved getting visits from her, and didn't care if it meant me not living to be a hundred; he knew she was the one for me to marry. She fit right into our visits. My wife's name is Jessalyn. She is what my mom describes as a beautiful southern belle. Mr. Rigney absolutely loved her. If she couldn't visit with me, he never let me stay long. He said I needed to go back home and tend to my woman's needs. He would jokingly say if I stayed too long visiting him, she would realize how ugly I am and leave while she could.

He always kept my picture in his wallet and claimed it was his security system. If someone ever stole his wallet, they would open it up, see my horrifying picture and drop it. It was one of his favorite jokes. Mr. Rigney knew that as Jessalyn and I got deeper into our relationship, it meant some of my weekend visits would be with her and not him. That never bothered him; he said it was the way it was supposed to be, and he didn't want it any other way.

By the time he passed, I was very happy that they had plenty of time to form their own relationship. He loved her, and Jessalyn loved him. He was one of the people I was most excited to tell when I decided to propose to Jessalyn. I remember taking him the ring I planned to give her when we got engaged. He looked down, staring at the diamond ring, speechless with how proud he was of Jess and me. He was a proud grandpa.

My wife loved him and helped me cope with losing Mr. Rigney better than I thought was possible at the time. She points out to me when she thinks he would be proud of me, and she holds me to the same standard of morality that Mr. Rigney lived by. Some of my favorite visits were with my wife. He made her feel so welcome to a family that, by blood, wasn't even his. She was his girl just as much as I was his boy. I will forever cherish the fact that they had a relationship. She got to see and meet the person behind the name.

His proudest moment for me personally came when I graduated from college. It is when I got my official nickname or my second official nickname. Now he referred to me as "My Boy" and "The Teacher." I graduated from Western Carolina University in the winter of 2016 with a dual degree in Special Education and Elementary Education and started my first teaching job less than one week later at JV Washam Elementary School teaching fifth grade. Mr. Rigney was there in spirit every step of the way. He never wanted me to come visit while I was away at college.

He wanted me to stay and focus on my studies as much as possible. That way, I could be the best teacher I could be. Western Carolina was about four hours away, so it was a haul to go and see him, but I always made sure to go see him on breaks and over the summer. Our visits weren't impacted too much by college.

Looking back on it, Mr. Rigney was right. I remember some more decent advice he gave me. He said, "When you get married, don't go and buy a bunch of stuff you can't afford. Buy stuff you can afford and improve as you go. This way, it will be yours, and you can be proud." Strangely enough, I followed his instructions when I did finally purchase a home of my own.

I never got to see Mr. Rigney in action. I do have one extremely vague memory of going to see Mr. Rigney at Patrick County High School when I was a toddler. That was the location where my mom met Mr. Rigney, and they forged their relationship. When we went this time, the school year was over, and all the desks were stacked for the school cleaning over the summer. I am not sure why we went or what we did after, but I do find peace in the fact that I did get to see Mr. Rigney in his happy place even if it is a minuscule memory.

Mr. Rigney forgot more about teaching than I will probably ever know. I viewed him as a pioneer. He learned how to teach from the ground up. He had no idea what a classroom was supposed to look like because he never completed school. He created what he thought it should be. He created an environment where everyone was welcome. It didn't matter who you were, what race, how smart, or how motivated you were as long as you wanted to learn. From what I could tell, this was never a problem because Mr. Rigney taught students how to fall in love with learning and feel successful. He always said, "All you have to do is meet them at their level," and he believed that was his key to success.

Mr. Rigney loved to teach, much like I realized early on. He was the #1 overall draft pick if this were sports, and without a doubt, he is a Hall of Famer. It was what he loved to do. I can totally relate currently because I want to go back to school and get my master's degree in school psychology. Mr. Rigney knew this was also a dream of mine, and he thought it was perfect for me.

Mr. Rigney once, or maybe like 1,300 times, told me a story of how he got promoted to be an administrator. He got a position at the central office for the school system, a fancy new job title, and probably a hefty raise. He did not even make it two weeks into that job before he headed back to the classroom. He couldn't do what he wanted to behind a desk or playing politics. Mr. Rigney pulled up his sleeves and got in the trenches, changing the world one student at a time. And that is the same feeling I got last year when I called a college about their school psychology program, and they informed me I would have to quit teaching to join. Teaching for us is a love that is scary to think of not having.

I loved listening to his stories about how he would go above and beyond his normal school role. For example, he always had bus duty. Nobody needed to tell him, and it was not always assigned to him, but if it was the end of the day, he wanted to be on the bus lot during dismissal sending those kids home. He was also the voice that male students heard read their names during high school commencement. He took that job super seriously. He believed this could be the most important moment of his students' lives, so he treated it that way in preparation and delivery.

He told me once that he would pay for an extra lunch every day so that he could give it to a student or join them if they needed a friend. He always ate lunch with his students or with the custodians

. He led many clubs. Someone once told me he led the forensics and debate team. He knew nothing about it, but a student wanted a club, and he was willing to be the sponsor.

I realized Mr. Rigney was an amazing teacher for intangible reasons. Not because he was the smartest person in the room (although he probably was), but because he had the biggest heart. I think I saw a lot of his teaching play out through my mom. I remember my mom telling me about her day of teaching at the high school where I attended.

We lived in Charlotte, and she taught students with behavior disorders. My mom taught some scary, bad people. But they were scared of her or respected her to the point that she thought they were a soft teddy bear while a lot of other teachers would have referred to them as thugs. She had a student show up to her class drunk off potato vodka. Tells you how country my mom is, she could smell potato vodka. Either way, she reported the student and told him what would then be happening. He was escorted by a police officer named Bautista, who was the most intimidating short man I had ever seen.

My mom followed them into the principal's office, where he admitted wrongdoing and was then asked to empty his pockets. After refusing, he was thrown to the floor, and a white bandana was taken from his pocket. In Charlotte, this was a sign that you were not affiliated with a gang and, therefore, did not want to take part in violence. It was protection if anything.

My mom was extremely unhappy with the violent treatment her student received and even tried to intervene with the police officer. The vice-principal and police officer warned Mom what she was doing could end poorly for her. She didn't care. I believe she would've gone to jail that day before watching two grown men cause physical harm to this teenager.

Regardless of what her student had done wrong, my mom took what Mr. Rigney had taught her and put it into practice at one of the scariest high schools in Charlotte, NC. Good teaching can take place anywhere; you just have to have a teacher that is willing to stand up for the right thing and always on the side of their students.

Mr. Rigney was lucky because he got to see his students go full circle. It wasn't all good, because if you're a teacher, you know that you can't save them all. But he had some success stories. There is not a profession in the world that Mr. Rigney has not taught someone involved. The man who lived in a hut helped produce everything from millionaire businessman to small-town farmers and woodcutters. I hope that one day when someone names a profession, I can think of a former student who does that. I currently teach fourth grade and have for four years. My oldest students are in the eighth grade. Only time will tell.

A brand new tattoo was placed on Rigney Marcela's arm on June 7, 2020, commemorating Mr. Rigney's birthday. He would have been 88.

Braxton Marcela, left, and Rigney Marcela, right at Braxton's graduation from Washington School of Law at American University.

A Kindergartner's Point of View

My oldest son, Braxton Marcela, wrote the following chapter. While he was not as close to Mr. Rigney as his brother was, they did have a relationship with each other that started when Braxton was in kindergarten.

I can barely remember a time when I did not know Mr. Rigney. In my kindergarten and first grade years of school, I saw him every morning before I got on the bus that went from Patrick County High School to Stuart Elementary School. Truth be told and tell it he did, I was not keen on going to school in my early years. I can't remember why exactly I was not a fan of it, but I wasn't. And, with cliché kindergartner naiveté, I complained and whined every morning about going—to my mom's chagrin and to Mr. Rigney's amusement. He claimed that I once rolled around on the floor, not wanting to go, something that neither my mom nor I remember, but he remembered. We didn't question it further.

I remember going to his classroom with my mom after the bus drove me back to Patrick County High School, probably in a better mood than in the morning. I would learn later that he always enjoyed seeing me when I came by. He never forgot those days, even though I certainly wished that he would. After I graduated from Hampden-Sydney College and then from American University Washington College of Law, he would say that he just could not believe that "that little boy who whined about not wanting to go to school would become so smart and educated."

As I grew up, I came to love literature and still do. My first exposure to classic literature came from my spare time as I waited for my mom to finish her teaching day at Patrick County High. I spent that time looking into some of her teaching materials for Shakespeare. For example, my mom had these shortened, cartoon videos of Shakespearean works. I remember watching *Romeo and Juliet* repeatedly and then making my way through *A Midsummer Night's Dream*.

Patrick County High also had mural paintings of various literary figures on the walls, including the witches in Shakespeare's *Macbeth*, Mark Twain, and Emily Dickinson, among others. When I went back to Patrick County High School for Mr. Rigney's memorial, these murals sparked my memory immediately.

I remember that as a child, I enjoyed a Disney movie called *Tom and Huck* loosely based on Mark Twain's characters Tom Sawyer and Huckleberry Finn. Disney didn't follow Mark Twain's storyline. I do remember talking to Mr. Rigney about the movie, and he must have found my interest amusing, given Mark Twain's books *The Adventures of*

Huckleberry Finn and *The Adventures of Tom Sawyer* are complicated novels exploring deep themes about southern-American culture, history, racial relations, and socioeconomic class. Both are far from being fully comprehensible to a kindergartner. He was teaching them to his high school students. He was patient with me though. He listened to me talk about the characters as I saw them in the movie, not as he knew them from Mark Twain's writing.

He even showed me a slide deck of illustrations of the characters from some of his teaching materials, which resembled Disney's casting. I later found the slides sitting in my mom's classroom and went through the deck with her. I wouldn't read either book until middle school or high school. When I did, I remembered sitting in his classroom and going through those slides. I can imagine that his actual teaching of those books would have been incredible. I may have been his youngest and most unconventional literature pupil, but the "lessons" stuck, and my interest in literature would manifest long after my days of dreading kindergarten.

I have sporadic memories of Mr. Rigney in my years between kindergarten and college. We would see him occasionally, mostly during some of our occasional trips from Charlotte, NC to Mount Airy, NC. I do always remember him being a part of our lives though, and somebody we always knew and who knew us. We would visit him before our family Christmas party every year, either meeting in the parking lot of a Food Lion in Mount Airy, North Carolina, or driving to his family's home in the mountains. When we visited his family's home, my brother and I spent most of the time playing outside and walking around observing the farm animals, many of which were old and kept their distance from us two obnoxious boys. We always found the mountains beautiful and enjoyed the trip.

We visited much more regularly after the frostbite and the medical issues. It seemed he was more accessible and more receptive to company.

I remember we went to see Mr. Rigney both right after I graduated high school, and right before I left for college. I attended Hampden-Sydney College, a small all-male college in rural Virginia. Mr. Rigney knew of it, and in all likelihood, probably taught one or two students who went there. He was probably surprised that I was going there because it was then, and is now a politically conservative school, yet I was a liberal Democrat from Charlotte, North Carolina. Mr. Rigney was a Democrat from Patrick County, so we got to have a few good laughs at Virginia politics and national politics. He started to call me "The Government Boy" because my mom talked about how much I liked politics. Mr.

Rigney remembered political events going back almost a century, and he read the newspaper every day.

Specifically, we got many laughs about former Virginia Attorney General Mary Sue Terry, the first woman elected statewide in Virginia. She had unsuccessfully run for governor and then retired to her home in Patrick County. She took a special interest in the school system and became somewhat of a bother to the Patrick County School Board. In Mr. Rigney's presence, her name was followed by an "Oh Lord..."

He took a special interest in talking about the state and national elections with me. He remembered former Virginia Governor Doug Wilder favorably. He concluded that Senator John McCain chose Sarah Palin to be his Vice-Presidential nominee because "that man didn't want to be President, and he started to have a chance and had to do something to stop that from happening."

He was fascinated and impressed by President Obama and was excited to discuss my experience working for the Obama 2012 campaign when I visited him in December 2012. He had choice words for both former Virginia Attorney General Ken Cuccinelli and former Governor Terry McAuliffe, who ran against each other in 2013. Mr. Rigney kept a letter signed by President Bill Clinton, congratulating him for his retirement after fifty years of teaching, framed right beside his prized Radford University degrees.

Getting back to Hampden-Sydney, Mr. Rigney was always proud of my accomplishments. He loved hearing about my college times as well. He even read a good portion of a book entitled *On this Hill*, written by Douglass Brinkley, about the history of Hampden-Sydney and told my mom all about his reading. After I graduated, he kept a printed copy of my Hampden-Sydney College degree, as well as a translation from its Latin print, on his wall among all the pictures of the friends whom he had told about "Ms. Honeycutt's Government Boy."

During the times I would visit, we would continue to talk about politics and my time in Washington, D.C. at American University Washington College of Law. He was fascinated by my time there. He was glad to see that I was learning and excited about going to school. He kept reminding me that I hated school when I was little.

I came to realize that he took a lot of pride in seeing my intellectual growth. He probably saw it as a key part of the close bonds that he would form with my brother and me. After my law school graduation, I spent weeks preparing for the North Carolina Bar Exam. My mom told him all about my study routine and our upcoming trip to

Raleigh, North Carolina, for the most difficult exam, and harrowing sixteen hours of my life so far. The week before the exam, he told my mom, "Ms. Honeycutt, I'm nervous. He's got that big test. I'm feeling it."

He wasn't alone. My mom told me about one of my aunts who woke up at 5:30 A.M. to pray for my passage of the bar exam. I imagine that Mr. Rigney read the newspaper chewed his Red Man tobacco, watched Ridiculousness (an MTV program that shows videos of people falling and doing stupid things), and thought about the anxiety he and I felt. Part of his nervousness came from his reading of bar exam statistics indicating that only 49% of examinees had passed it on the first administration the previous year.

When I learned two months later that I had passed the bar exam, my mom called Brenda Kay and told her simply to tell Mr. Rigney, "He passed the test. He'll know what that means." He was elated. And me, I was promoted; he would call me "The Lawyer." From then on, after every visit, he would tell his friends that "The Lawyer" visited. At his memorial, I noted that most people don't brag about getting visited by a lawyer, but Mr. Rigney did.

Mr. Rigney's admiration and love for us was deep and profound, even if he never verbally expressed it explicitly. It was apparent to us. When my mom told him that I was joining the Army Judge Advocate General's Corps, she told me that he got really quiet and said, "Ms. Honeycutt, I don't like this very much." My mom explained that I was going to be a lawyer and was not likely going to be in direct combat. This seemed to comfort him, but he internalized that worry. I couldn't be surprised.

He was a child during the Second World War and began teaching during the Korean War. He remembered the assassination of John F. Kennedy (he was probably teaching on that Friday afternoon in 1963). He taught students who received their draft cards to go to Vietnam. Some probably did not return. He remembered the swaths of history that I had only studied. He had watched and read about my generation's fighting in the Global War on Terror, which began when I was ten years old, and he had retired from teaching. I remember visiting him after my graduation from Officer Basic Course, and he was proud but still maintained that nervousness. My mom had given him pictures of me in my uniform.

There's a lot to be said about the grandfatherly relationship he had with both my brother and me. He took great pride in supporting us and getting to see us grow throughout our own personal and educational journeys.

During my visits to the nursing home, he would tell my mom and me about the visitors and nurses that he was interacting with. He enjoyed seeing and speaking with us, and he always gave us a good laugh.

His connection to my brother was stronger, not just because my brother is his namesake, but I was frequently away at school. I didn't get to visit as often as the rest of my family, and I never visited on my own without my mom or my brother. He still always loved it when I would come. He always had plenty of things to talk about, whether it was history, people he had met, or his old teaching stories.

I always knew how much he meant to my mother. She once gave me a long explanation during one of our trips to the motel-apartment, going back to when they first met. I believe she told me this to explain why she visited so frequently and took off so many days from work, often at her own expense, and costing almost all of her allotted sick days. She talked about how much his friendship and mentorship meant to her and why she would do whatever it took to help him through his health struggles. I listened to the explanation, but my mom certainly didn't owe me an explanation. Her sacrifices for Mr. Rigney did not require a justification beyond what I already knew of their relationship. I knew that she didn't begrudge a minute of the time or expense.

She had a successful teaching career, surely attributable to his mentorship, so the expenses of a couple of sick days didn't matter. I knew and understood her commitment to him. I understood that she was paying forward years of mentorship and his years of being a fixture in our lives.

Their friendship alluded to their early days as mentor-mentee. She never called him George. He never called her Marsha (or Marshalene). He never even called her Mrs. Marcela, only referring to her as Ms. Honeycutt, her maiden name. I saw this clearly, and I admired it.

I also saw the impact that Mr. Rigney had on my brother, his namesake, and "My Boy." I was always "The Government Boy," "The Jewish (Juris) Doctor," or "The Lawyer." My brother was Mr. Rigney's "My Boy."

Mr. Rigney grew to be my brother's best friend and as strong a mentor to him as he had been for my mother. I never quite realized this until the memorial. My brother loved visiting him and drove his friends out to see Mr. Rigney. For Rigney's friends, they were going to see "the original Rigney." Many of Rigney's friends earned a spot on Mr. Rigney's wall.

He drove Mr. Rigney on similar excursions to those my mother took him on to see his old friends and acquaintances. They would talk for hours. My brother took Jessalyn to meet Mr. Rigney only after she had met us and gotten our approval with flying colors. Rigney knew from the earliest of my memories that he was destined to be a teacher, just like the man for whom he was named. And my brother is a damn good teacher. I've heard so many stories about how his students love and admire him. I've seen my brother care for his students in a profound way. For example, he learned that he was going to have a student that was battling childhood cancer, so he immediately bought and read books about teaching severely ill students—he did this work for only one of his students.

My brother was never very politically opinionated, but as soon as he had a transgender student in his class for a semester, he became animated in his support for gay and transgender rights in education and lost any patience he had for intolerance. He has shown me the creativity that he has used in his classroom, and I have seen the way his students respond to him. This is clearly a reflection of Mr. Rigney and their long conversations, often on an overlook watching an alpaca farm or eating Burger King.

I had not realized just how strongly Mr. Rigney touched and motivated my brother and his career. It is powerful to see that Mr. Rigney's career has now taken new life in Rigney Marcela's career. He made my brother who he is today professionally. I'm grateful that he was able to provide his namesake with that motivation and mentorship that is now shaping and motivating children once again.

On the day that Mr. Rigney began his journey to his final rest, I was moving into a new house. I had been working for a private law firm that had paid me just enough resources to purchase a small bungalow in an overpriced western North Carolina housing market. Mr. Rigney knew this because my mom had visited him just shortly before and told him of the house. My mom got "the call" and left the moving to me. My brother had visited that day, and both he and Jessalyn knew "the call" was coming. My mom got "the call" and left. She didn't ask me to go with her. I was surprised that she didn't ask, and I would have gone if she did. I think we both figured he would have wanted me to finish moving in.

He was proud that I was able to purchase the house and proud of my new legal career. I also assumed, at least partly, that my mom wanted to say goodbye to her mentor alone and didn't want me there to see that moment and whatever vulnerability that it carried. I understood that and didn't ask if she wanted me to go. My dad finished unloading the truck and proceeded to join my mom at the hospital.

The next day, I got the call from my mom that Mr. Rigney had passed peacefully and quietly. An important and specific chapter in her life closed. An important and specific chapter in my brother's life closed. For me, I felt like even if I didn't have a full chapter of my life that pointed to Mr. Rigney, he was a part of every chapter that my life had written. He was there for every big moment and smiled at every development—from "that boy who didn't want to go to school" to "The Government Boy" to "The Jewish Doctor" to "The Lawyer." I later learned that "The Lawyer" was one of the last words Mr. Rigney said. In his last moments, he thought of me as well.

He saw his "Boy" and his "Boy's Wife." He saw Ms. Honeycutt and my dad, Mike. My mom assured him that I was well. He passed knowing that even if he did not see me then, he had seen me through so many years and so many stages. He had seen so many versions of me, and "The Lawyer" was the one that he left behind. His work in my life too had been successful, and he knew it as he passed.

When I spoke at Mr. Rigney's memorial service, I talked about how he taught and shared his insight and wisdom with others. Literature, I stated then, is full of various characters who sought to find themselves with varying degrees of success. Mark Twain wrote about characters who tried to find themselves and their place in a racially divided and volatile South. My favorite novel, J.D. Salinger's *A Catcher in the Rye* is all about a character's search for himself. Mr. Rigney knew these titles well and probably had taught them at some point.

Mr. Rigney's self was simple, and one word—teacher. Both in the classroom and out, he taught. He learned. He read. He inspired, and he motivated. He watched as the products of his teaching grew and fulfilled the very promise that education and enlightenment provide us. While I'm still finding my "self," I am incredibly grateful for my relationship with Mr. Rigney and the guidance he gave me.

My mom once told me that during one of her visits with Mr. Rigney, there came a point in the conversation in which he randomly, and without any context, looked up and said, "You know, Thomas Jefferson was an idiot." I can imagine that this left my mom stunned and a bit amused, given Jefferson is regarded with such esteem as one of America's prominent political thinkers, writers, founding fathers, and presidents. As a student of history, I could have understood his point, as Jefferson's life practices often contradicted his writings, especially with regards to slavery. Personally, I prefer his contemporary Alexander Hamilton. However, to Mr. Rigney, Jefferson's idiocy was simple, and it had everything to do with my brother and me, and nothing to do with the historians' views on Jefferson.

Knowing that such an intelligent mind would have an answer for such a blunt statement, my mom asked Mr. Rigney, "Why do you say that Jefferson was an idiot?" Mr. Rigney smiled and said, "He said that all men were created equal, and I've seen your boys and that just isn't true. They're just great boys, and they're smarter and had more opportunities than some of these other people."

Mr. Rigney's point, however, was not about elitism or even condescension to others. His love of civil rights and human dignity is well-expressed and detailed by the other chapters of this novel. The takeaway from his statement was about how he had seen my brother and me grow up into adults. He had watched my parents, especially my mom, raise us to be successful and caring adults. Among the countless people he knew and came across, we stood out to him as being finished products that stood out above many others.

He was truly correct that not all men and not all selves are created equal. Some people pass with the time and are remembered scantly, and some people live vicariously through well-earned legacies. Mr. Rigney

rests in the latter. He shaped and was shaped by the people he taught and

the people he inspired. I'm glad that he was able to have been a part of

my own and my family's lives.

Frostbite Surgery

His doctors said, "Frostbite in January; amputation in July," so I expected Mr. Rigney to be in the nursing home until July before there would be any discussion of surgery. I had asked his nephew to make arrangements with the nursing home staff for me to pick him up and take him to Baptist Hospital for his regular appointments. We started out going about every week.

I was surely surprised in mid-February 2011, only six weeks after being discharged from the hospital when the surgeon looked at his frostbitten feet and said he had healed as much as possible, and he was now ready for amputations. I couldn't believe that he was five months ahead of schedule, but he was.

Fortunately for me, my principal was very supportive and told me to take all the time I needed for him. When I took him for his pre-op session a few days before the actual surgery, we had to complete quite a bit of paperwork, which was very time consuming. He was attended by a very old nurse who didn't have much personality. He kept shaking his head and repeating "inefficient, inefficient" as she walked in and out. After signing one of the forms giving his consent for surgery, he looked at his shaky handwriting and said, "Look at that. I can't write like I used to."

I felt very sad when he showed me his squiggly signature. His letters were still perfectly formed, but they were written by a shaky hand. Given that he had been a handwriting teacher, his perfect handwriting had always been a source of pride for him.

We ended up sitting in an exam room for long periods between visits from staff personnel who were making preparations for his surgery. He told me various stories during those times--things that I hadn't known before.

The story I remember most clearly from that day was about his romance with my second-grade schoolteacher. Based on what he told me, she had been in love with him and wanted to get married. Although he was reluctant to admit it, I concluded that he loved her too. He insisted, however, that he didn't feel like marriage was right for them because she lived in town.

He said, "I knew she would never survive the mountain life that I lived and loved, and I was positive there was no way I could live in town. She had far too much money to make me happy."

She did indeed come from a wealthy family. I am not sure what the actual source of her family wealth was, but she had a lifelong career as a schoolteacher. Neither she nor Mr. Rigney ever married.

While that is intriguing, the part of the love story that moved me the most was about her death in 1984. She was in her mid-sixties when she died. I was just starting to know Mr. Rigney when it happened, and I can remember him mentioning it to me at the time as he knew I had attended the school where she taught--and where he had once taught as well. I didn't know that they had been involved in a relationship, and I told him how mean she was to us. He said he knew she was a mean teacher, but I would never have said that if I had known they had been an item.

As we sat in the hospital room that day, he elaborated on the effect her death had on him. He told me that he chose not to go see her at the funeral home. Mr. Rigney didn't see a reason to at that time; however, he told me that he had spoken with a former colleague, who had attended the visitation.

She told Mr. Rigney that his former girlfriend was buried wearing "the necklace you gave her for Christmas all those years ago."

He said, "I paid $6 for the necklace at Randleman Drug Store" in Mount Airy.

It was then that I realized how serious their relationship had been. I wonder if she pined away for him all those years. Maybe that's why she was so mean to her students.

We got through the pre-op process eventually that day and would return to the hospital two days later for the actual amputations. I arrived at the nursing home to pick him up only to find him scared to death. He was in a total state of dread throughout the entire drive from Patrick County to Winston Salem.

He repeatedly said, "I know what it feels like to go to one's own execution."

I tried to reassure him as we traveled. I jokingly said, "They aren't going to kill you--just take off your leg."

Even humor didn't assuage his fears, but he would at least try to laugh a little. He also made clear to me that it was not the amputations that scared him:

"I'm afraid I will never wake up from the anesthesia, and I'll just lie like a vegetable for the rest of my life."

I tried to tell him that it was rare for this to happen, but he kept saying he knew someone who had that experience. He repeated these fears all the way to the hospital and continued after we got there.

His surgery was scheduled for the early afternoon. We were very much on time--even early. We got him checked in, and he was placed in a "holding" room waiting for his surgery. Unbeknown to us, there was a huge emergency involving a fire, and the surgeons had to give their attention to the victim, leaving us in that room for hours. He was lying on the hospital bed repeating how scared he was.

When the doctor came in, he asked if he had to be put to sleep. The doctor responded, "No, you can be administered an epidural and stay awake for the whole process."

I asked some questions because I wasn't sure he could tolerate seeing what was going to happen. The surgeon said they would place a panel in front of his face so he couldn't see anything. Since he was so hard of hearing, I knew he couldn't hear the process or what the surgeons were saying. The doctors also told me that they would give him several drugs to keep him relaxed during the procedure. He bravely went through the amputations without going under anesthesia.

His surgery was brief and successful. I waited in the surgical waiting room while Dr. James Holmes performed the amputations. He called me on a hospital phone to let me know progress at various intervals.

Once it was over, he came and sat with me and explained the procedure and the healing process.

He told me that all humans have three veins in their thigh that extend into the calf of the leg. At the approximate age of 55, the veins all join together, forming one large vein. He said that Mr. Rigney still had all three veins intact. He compared his leg to that of a college athlete, and he asked me how Mr. Rigney had stayed in such great physical shape.

I told him that he had cut and loaded timber with his nephews in Fancy Gap, Virginia. The mention of Fancy Gap piqued Dr. Holmes's interest, and he told me he had a friend from Fancy Gap who had donated the funding for the Burn Unit, where Mr. Rigney's frostbite was being treated. When he told me the friend's last name was Meredith, I explained that Mr. Rigney had lived with a family of that name when he attended Radford University. Strangely enough, the donor was a relative of the family he had lived with all those years ago.

I recently learned that the donor is a doctor who owns a summer home about one-fourth mile from Mr. Rigney's gravesite. They had been neighbors.

Dr. Holmes told me where to go to wait for the nurses to get Mr. Rigney to his room. While waiting, I found a book about the famous Flat

Rock School fire in the early 1960's. I knew the book existed, but I had never seen a copy of it. My sisters and brother had been students at Flat Rock School when it burned. While they and most of the students got out safely, one student and one teacher died. Several other students were badly burned and scarred as a result of the fire.

Mr. Rigney was not a teacher at Flat Rock when the fire occurred, but his former girlfriend was. Her picture and her thoughts about the fire were in the book, along with pictures of many other teachers.

Once he was finally situated in his room, I asked him if he wanted me to spend the night. He had been through a traumatic experience, but he was alert and extremely talkative--the drugs were alleviating his pain. He asked me if I thought Mike, my husband, would mind. I assured him that Mike didn't care, so I settled into one of the hospital's sleeping chairs and attempted to go to sleep.

Mr. Rigney's pain medications continued to keep him awake and energetic, thereby limiting my opportunities for sleep. We were also constantly interrupted by attending nurses and other personnel who were coming in to monitor Mr. Rigney. The few occasions upon which I did fall asleep were brief because Mr. Rigney would start a new conversation each time. He constantly thanked me for being there and kept telling me

111

he was going to pay me. I told him he had already paid me throughout the years; this was just my opportunity to pay him back.

He made the bold statement that he was paying me even if "I have to get a job."

I said, "Yes, Mr. Rigney, there are many places that will hire an 80-year old man with one leg."

We laughed, but he seriously wanted to pay me as he never wanted to feel indebted to anyone for anything. I never accepted money from him for the time I spent with him before, during, or after his surgery.

After his surgery, I had brought the book about the fire back to his room so he could look at it when he felt up to it. The day after his surgery, he went through the book page by page explaining to me who each of the teachers were. I already knew most of them because they were still on staff at Flat Rock School when I was a student there.

That book would never be returned to the waiting room. Not only did he take the book with him, but he had all the attending healthcare professionals sign it before he left the hospital. No one ever questioned that we were taking something that didn't belong to us; the staff wanted him to have that book.

Over the next few days, various healthcare professionals came into Mr. Rigney's room. They got him up and made him walk, or hop, with a walker the morning after his surgery. They immediately scheduled physical therapy, and he willingly participated on a regular basis.

He had so much he had to learn to do before he could be fitted for a prosthetic leg, including an additional surgery during which they would graft skin from his hip to repair the damage to his remaining foot where all five toes had been removed. He took all this in stride and was hopping on his bandaged foot behind his walker. He never complained about the inevitable pain, including phantom pains.

After several days, plans were made for his return to the nursing home, where he would receive intense rehabilitation. Since he was closely monitored, he had to go in an ambulance instead of by car. He seemed to be okay with that idea, so he told me to go back home and return to work. I worried about him being alone during his return to the nursing home, but it worked out fine as he was quite entertained by the two young men who transported him. It appeared that the ambulance driver and his partner communicated with him throughout the entire drive back to Patrick County.

Once he was back in the nursing home, we resumed our weekly and eventual bi-weekly drives to Baptist Hospital for his check-ins with his doctors. I enjoyed that time with him as we had great conversations. I could also take him for rides allowing him to see the beautiful mountains with their oncoming spring blossoms.

During his time of healing and rehabilitation, Meadows of Dan Elementary School burned. I drove him up to see the ruins on the way back to the nursing home from one of our hospital visits.

After the amputations, it was a great struggle getting him in and out of the car. This would improve as he continued his physical therapy because he quickly developed great strength in his upper body. He could then hold onto the top of the car and help me with the transfer. One chilly morning when I went to pick him up at the nursing home for a hospital visit, Mark Barnwell, a nursing assistant and a former student, walked out with us. When Mark saw us struggling, he effortlessly picked up Mr. Rigney and sat him in the car seat. Mr. Rigney was smiling and thanking Mark. He looked so small in Mark's big muscular arms.

Since my spring break from school was scheduled during April, I went ahead and asked the surgeons to schedule his skin grafts for that week. We once again retreated to Baptist hospital. Never having had a skin graft, I didn't know the seriousness of the surgery, but he was in quite

a bit of pain after this procedure. He also had a device connected to his

foot that was supposed to pump out any infectious materials. He still took

this all in stride and rarely, if ever, complained. Once again, he had to be

transported to the nursing home in an ambulance.

Mr. Rigney is shown seated on the front row at a reunion with his colleagues, who were all part of the original Patrick County High School staff when the school opened in 1970. This picture was taken shortly after his amputation. This picture of Patrick County High School Faculty and Staff in the 1970s was taken at an anniversary dinner for the first faculty of PCHS. The picture was taken in May 2011 at the building expansion dedication. Seated left to right: Jo Moricle, Beatrice Wood, Lennis Inman, George Rigney, Priscilla Diggs, and Rickie Shores. Row 1, L – R, John Shore, Ann Belcher, Jimmy Mitchell. Mack George, Algie Spencer, Ella Sue Joyce Goard, Sonny Swails, Polly Tatum, Jane Akers, Jane Smith Ford, Charlene Lawson, Carolyn Williams, Cindy Agnes Stovall, Joyce Hall, Phyllis Eastridge, John Halsey, Mary Lee Mitchell, Cindy Griffith, Evelyn Hazelwood, Barbara Pendleton. Back Row, L-R, John Shore, Bruce Dollarhite, Richard Tobler, Clarence Hall, Fred Brim, James K. Hiatt, Principal, John Weatherman, Asst. Principal. Also present, but not in the picture were Laura Flippin and Bill Hanner.

Prosthetic Leg

Despite the pain, his skin grafts healed quickly, and we were able to get him fitted for his prosthetic leg. He was extremely excited and convinced that once it was put on, he would be able to walk normally. He didn't realize that he would have to have daily rehabilitation before efficiently using the limb. I had been busy giving end-of-grade tests on the day he was expected to receive his prosthetic, so my husband Mike took him to the clinic. Mike reported that Mr. Rigney was extraordinarily excited about getting the leg, and he was anticipating walking out of the clinic unassisted.

He kept telling Mike that the prosthetist had said, "It will just become a part of you." I had indeed heard her tell him that in subsequent visits, but Mr. Rigney would leave out her final two words- "over time" – whenever he talked about his new leg. Walking unassisted didn't happen for him that day, but he was quite successful on the parallel bars. Having to go back to the car in a wheelchair was a huge disappointment to him, but he took it all in stride.

He actively engaged in his physical therapy, so it was not long before he could walk using his walker. He constantly walked up and down the halls at the nursing home, making friends, not just with other residents, but with visitors who had come to see the other residents. He had a daily entourage of visitors, most of them former students and colleagues, to all of whom he wanted to show off his "fake leg" and walking skills. This desire to show off his walking increased once he graduated to walking with a cane. He made progress so quickly and always kept his positive outlook.

His physical therapists and doctors couldn't say enough about his hard work during physical therapy sessions. His prosthetist once said, "You do everything I tell you to do. I wish all my patients would."

After about a year, she said she had done all she could do to help him because he had followed all her instructions and could handle his walking on his own. He questioned this because he wanted to be able to walk without a cane or walker. He asked, "Why can't I walk as well as that man in the waiting area who has a fake leg?" She pointed out that the man was about forty years old.

His physical therapy was also terminated at the nursing home, but he continued to live there for several months longer. He kept hinting that he wanted to go home, but since his house had burned down before his initial hospitalization, I really didn't think his family would agree to his being discharged from the nursing home, but I was surely wrong.

Leaving the Nursing Home

In March of 2012, I called the nursing home to let them know that I would be taking Mr. Rigney to a doctor's appointment the next day. The attendant who answered the phone told me that he no longer lived there and had been gone for well over a week. Because of confidentiality privileges, she could not give me any details.

I called Junebug, his nephew, that night, and he explained that Mr. Rigney had arranged with him to be picked up and taken to an old motel, which was now used as a boarding house. It was located in Hillsville, Virginia. Junebug assured me that he would be safe living there for the time being.

I was very worried, but since I didn't have any legal rights to his care, there was nothing I could do, and it was a family decision. Junebug put most of my worries to rest when he further explained that he would be visiting Mr. Rigney every morning at breakfast and again before bedtime. True to his word, he did this every day and night until his own illness would no longer allow it.

During the day, Brenda Kaye, Mr. Rigney's niece, would be checking in with him. At first, she spent much of each morning driving him to various stores and just taking him for rides. Brenda would be the person who shopped for most of his groceries, tobacco, and newspapers. She had also agreed to clean his room and do his laundry, which she did in the beginning, but he soon relieved her of those chores, and I took them over.

In a phone conversation, I asked Junebug to tell Mr. Rigney that I would be visiting him the following Saturday. When I arrived, he and Brenda Kaye were in the parking lot waiting for me.

I didn't know his plan, but he quickly informed me that he wanted to go for a ride. I had recently inherited a large 2002 Mercury Grand Marquis from my father-in-law, who had taken ill and died shortly after Mr. Rigney left the nursing home. Mr. Rigney was able to get in and out of the car independently. Brenda Kaye folded his walker and put it in the trunk. I helped him with his seatbelt, and we were on our way.

He said, "Blue Ridge Parkway South. We are going to an alpaca farm." I had no idea where this place was located, but he knew exactly, and he gave me very specific directions. The business was closed that day, but we could see alpacas from the parking lot located on the property.

The No Trespassing signs did not deter Mr. Rigney from insisting that we drive down to the barn so he could get a closer look. He always loved animals, and he was like a small child as he observed these animals at pasture. In the newspaper article about his 1999 retirement, he described himself as an "animal specialist." He loved all animals and had always taken care of as many as he could on his property.

We then got on the Parkway South and drove out to the site of one of his early teaching assignments, which was a white country church, known to him as Blue Ridge School. There were lots of people there working on the building, so he met the current minister and several of the parishioners. The building was not the original church where he taught as it had been torn down and replaced. There was, however, an historical marker where the original church had stood denoting the church's use as a school. Seeing this marker was thrilling for Mr. Rigney, so I took a picture of it for him.

We had a beautiful day together that Saturday. It was early spring, and the weather was perfect--or "ideal" as Mr. Rigney would have described it. This would be the first of many, many day trips that Mr. Rigney and I would take together. I visited him at least twice a month and more when I had time off from my teaching job. We would spend many Saturdays or Sundays going for long car rides and visiting his teacher friends.

During these visits with friends, I learned much about Mr. Rigney's life and career. Almost everyone we visited was very receptive of us, but some spent more time with him than others. I knew some of these people, but others I had never even heard of. I didn't know where they lived, and at first, I was not all that familiar with a GPS; however, it didn't take me all that long to learn that I needed to get a new phone that had one on it. Sometimes, I would just try to follow Mr. Rigney's directions, which could be sketchy, but usually led us to where he wanted to go.

Visit with Owen Bowman

In December 2012, I was scheduled to attend a birthday party in my hometown of Mount Airy, North Carolina. Since Mount Airy is located just a few miles south of Hillsville, Virginia, I left early that morning so that I could take Mr. Rigney out for a ride before the party. He told me that he wanted to visit an old friend, Owen Bowman, who lived in Lambsburg, Virginia, which is located right on the North Carolina/Virginia state line. Mr. Rigney said the gentleman was a former principal, and they had been friends many years ago. I had no idea who the man was or where he lived, but I knew that Judy, my sister, lived near Lambsburg, so I called her to see if she knew this gentleman, thinking perhaps that she could help me at least find the right road.

As it turned out, my sister's daughter, Tammy, was married to Mr. Bowman's grandson, Luke. Mr. Rigney's directions had taken me very close to the area of his home, so she gave me the specifics, and we were able to find him with little difficulty. After driving along several curvy mountain roads, we found the house nestled back in the woods. We crossed a small wooden, low-water bridge and arrived at what had once been a picturesque mountain home, but now needed some updating.

When I knocked on the door, he yelled, "Come in."

I was a little apprehensive about walking into a home of someone I had never met, but I opened the door and identified myself. Mr. Bowman was mobile, but old and quite feeble. As he stood, I noticed that he was stooped and used a hand-whittled cane. I explained that Mr. Rigney was in the car and unable to come inside, but would like for him to come out if he was able.

He grabbed his coat and kept repeating, "This is such a treat. I haven't seen George in years. What a treat!"

He made it to the car, and I helped him into the driver's seat. I took a seat in the back and let them visit. They talked so much about their lives dating back to their college days. Mr. Bowman and Mr. Rigney had both taught in the small, one-room schoolhouses, eventually making their way into the more modern schools. They discussed college courses, segregation, facilities, administrators, and most any other topic relating to public education. I wish I had brought a recorder, so I could have recorded all the history they were discussing.

Once Mr. Bowman had taught a class for the University of Virginia. I am not sure where they were living or working at that time, but he had a lengthy drive and didn't want to travel alone. He asked Mr. Rigney to enroll in the class. He promised him an "A" if he would just sign up for the class and go with him. In efforts to help his friend, Mr. Rigney enrolled in the class, and they traveled together. They discussed how much fun they had talking to each other and just enjoying each other's company during the rides.

Mr. Rigney kept telling Mr. Bowman, who was already married at the time, how much the female students in the class enjoyed having him as a teacher. Since the students knew the two men were friends, they asked Mr. Rigney what kind of gift they could get as a thank you to Mr. Bowman for teaching the class. Mr. Rigney told them that money was always the best gift, so the class took up a donation and presented it to Mr. Bowman.

They talked about education before the Civil Rights Movement. Mr. Rigney relayed a memory of a time when he rode a Greyhound bus from Wytheville, Virginia, to Radford College when he was a student. At that time, black people could only sit at the back of the bus after the white people had boarded and taken a seat. Mr. Rigney refused to get on the bus with the white people but stood outside with the black people. He struggled with the treatment the black riders experienced and once discussed it with the driver. The driver told him that there would come a time when this type of discrimination would end.

Being the liberal, open-minded thinker that he was, he was always quick to express his happiness that African-Americans gained their rights, but he continued to believe that they still weren't treated with the level of respect they should have.

This story transitioned to Mr. Bowman's account of a time that he hired a black woman to be his secretary in one of the schools he served in West Virginia.

He said, "George, the Ku Klux Klan came to my house and brought a cross. They gave me until the next day to fire her, and then they threatened my family."

He declared that he never thought her hiring would create a problem, "I hired her because she was a qualified, good worker. It never crossed my mind the trouble it would cause."

He refused to fire the lady, but he ended up leaving that school district because of this incident. He moved his family to Virginia, where his wife had a family. He never learned what happened to the secretary after she left school, but he did not fire her.

Both of these men believed in equal education and work privileges for everyone. They both spent many years investing in their education and the education of others, and neither of them saw race or economic status as a criteria for measuring their students.

Several years later, my son would make a statement at Mr. Rigney's memorial service regarding his acceptance of all students and how "he did not need the Supreme Court to tell him that a white child and a black child had the same rights to education or that separate but equal was not equal. He didn't need the Supreme Court to tell him that disabled children also had the right to a free and appropriate education. He taught the student in front him the best way he knew how."

As they continued to talk about their early days, they spoke of the one-room schoolhouses. Mr. Rigney talked about getting up early, walking to school, and starting early morning fires in the pot-bellied stoves to get the school warm for the kids. Since busing had not become a reality at that time, his students had to walk to school, so it was essential that the building be warm when they arrived.

He arrived at his school about 5 AM and, after getting the building warm and the firewood brought inside, he would work on his lessons for the day. It was his job to open, close, and maintain the building as there were no custodians or maintenance personnel for these facilities.

Mr. Bowman, in turn, told his story of working in a small public school that did not have custodians, so he asked the boys to take turns cleaning the restrooms and sweeping the floors. He reported that most of the boys willingly took a turn, but one day, a boy suggested that he take a turn.

After pondering this idea, he said, "I agree with you. I guess I should take a turn."

He placed his name on the rotation and began cleaning the restrooms when his turn came up.

This would not be the only time that we visited Mr. Bowman. We went back several times, and each visit was equally well-received and usually lasted several hours. I was never bored as I listened to all the history these two men shared and re-lived, so I was very saddened to hear that Mr. Bowman had a stroke in the fall of 2015.

The good news was that he was going to recover and return to his home. On January 16, 2016, Mr. Rigney asked that we check on Mr. Bowman at his home. He said he knew that he wasn't able to come out for a visit, but I should go in and see if he was recovering.

As instructed, I went into Mr. Bowman's home, where a neighbor was also visiting with him. The neighbor happened to know Mr. Rigney, so he went to the car and visited with him while I spent a few minutes with Mr. Bowman. He was sitting in his chair, surrounded by books and newspapers, smoking a cigar. My first thought was how easily a fire could ignite, and I wondered if he would even be able to get out.

He recognized me from previous visits, so I proceeded to tell him that Mr. Rigney wanted me to check on him. He responded that he was doing very well with his recovery. I was surprised that he was as strong and coherent as he was, as there had been some scary moments during his illness. He was also very lucid and appeared to have been affected very little by his stroke.

Mr. Bowman and I had an intellectual conversation about politics-- he was an avid supporter of President Obama and was reading one of his books. He had other books lying on the table next to him. I picked up a paperback copy of *The Count of Monte Cristo*. I asked him if he planned to read that book next. He said he had read it years ago but was going to read it again; it had been a previous Christmas gift from his late wife. We discussed that book and others before I excused myself and returned to my car.

Mr. Rigney was delighted to hear that Mr. Bowman had recovered and was avidly reading good literature. We left feeling good about the visit.

It was just a few hours later, as I was traveling to my home in Boone, North Carolina, that I got a phone call from my sister, Judy. She asked if I had visited Mr. Bowman earlier that day. I confirmed that I had and asked her how she knew. Before answering, she asked how his health had seemed that day. I told her that he was fine and seemed to be almost completely recovered from the stroke. She then informed me that he had been found slumped over his woodpile shortly after we left. It appeared that he had had another stroke or a heart attack.

Given that he was 91 years old, an autopsy would not be performed. The family felt it was safe to assume that he died of natural causes. After my shock subsided, I asked her again how she knew that I had been there, and she told me that he had written it down in the journal kept on the table beside his chair.

I had to take some time to process all that she had told me because, in addition to being shaken myself, I knew that Mr. Rigney had to be informed of Mr. Bowman's death. I was about halfway home and didn't feel comfortable turning around to go back to Hillsville as the weather channel was forecasting a snowstorm in Boone that night. I called Judy's daughter, Tammy, and her husband, Luke, who was Mr. Bowman's grandson and asked them if they could tell Mr. Rigney. They agreed to go to his apartment the next morning.

I fully expected him to be devastated when he heard the news, so I called his niece, Brenda Kaye, to let her know that Mr. Rigney was about to be informed of the loss of his dear, dear friend. She said she would check on him after they had time to tell him. When I called Brenda Kaye later, she said he took the news well but was finding it hard to believe since he had been so well when we were there earlier that day.

I visited Mr. Rigney the following Saturday to check on him. He told me all the details of Tammy and Luke's visit and how they had brought their most impressive children with them. They had brought him Mr. Bowman's copy of *The Count of Monte Cristo* as a gift. He was so pleased to have it and would later be gifted with much more of Mr. Bowman's reading materials, most of which were filled with historical information about his beloved Carroll County, Virginia. He kept these materials on a table beside his wheelchair, and he read and re-read from them until his death.

It would be a year or two later that Mr. Bowman's great-grandson, Nathan Golding, also my great-nephew, would graduate from North Surry High School. Mr. Rigney took him and his younger sister each a one-hundred dollar bill. He told me that was the last thing he could do for Mr. Bowman.

Random Visits

Occasionally, Mr. Rigney would get an idea that he wanted to visit someone who had come to the nursing home to preach, sing, or entertain in some capacity. One cloudy Saturday morning, we set out to find a minister he had previously met at the nursing home on a Sunday afternoon.

It is important to mention that Mr. Rigney had been gone from the nursing home for about five years when he decided we were going to find this minister. He carried the man's business card bearing his name and address—neither of which I can remember. Other than that, neither of us knew anything about this gentleman except that he was an African-American preacher, who lived in the Patrick Springs area.

So, using my GPS as a guide, we made our way to Patrick Springs, Virginia. We followed the directions to a nice little house with two tiny pink bicycles and other large outdoor toys strewn about the yard. I made the statement that he must have grandchildren because children were living at that house. I reluctantly went to knock on the door, not believing that we were at the right house. I felt a large sigh of relief when no one answered because I was spared having to introduce myself to a stranger who probably was not the person I was looking for.

When I told Mr. Rigney that no one was home, he instructed me to continue to drive on that same road as we might pass someone who could give us information about this preacher. As fate would have it, we passed a woman who was out for her morning walk. We stopped, and Mr. Rigney asked her if she knew this man and exactly which house was his. She offered her condolences and informed us that the minister had died four years earlier. As they were having a conversation about what a fine man the preacher had been, she realized that Mr. Rigney had taught her children.

While I have no idea who this woman was, she and Mr. Rigney realized they had once known each other quite well. When she realized who he was, she was so excited. She was trying to reach through the car windows to hug him. They reminisced about her children's experiences in his classes many years before. She assured him that he was a favorite of both her children,

As we continued on our way, Mr. Rigney remembered another person who lived in the same area. This gentleman, whose name he didn't recall--nor do I believe we ever learned--had come to the nursing home to play the accordion for the residents. Mr. Rigney didn't know exactly where he lived but knew it was in the vicinity of the former minister's house. He told me what road I should get on, which was easy because it was just a right turn from where we were.

I drove for what seemed like hours (but it was only about twenty or thirty minutes) until we came to the end of the long, curvy road. True to his word, Mr. Rigney identified the house where the gentleman with the accordion lived. I have no idea how he knew where to find this man. We did not have his business card or address.

Thankfully, this nice man was outside doing yard work, so I didn't have to appear at the stranger's door and ask if a man who played the accordion lived there. I got out of the car and introduced myself and told him that Mr. Rigney wanted to visit him. He didn't seem to know Mr. Rigney at all. I explained that they had met at the nursing home, but he still didn't remember him. He told me that he had not played his accordion at the nursing home for several years. I asked him to come to the car and see Mr. Rigney, and perhaps he would remember him.

Upon seeing him, he remembered him as the nursing home resident who was a former teacher who had lost his leg. The man greeted him and offered to bring out the accordion and play for him. He went inside and, after a few seconds, returned with the instrument and a music stand. He set the stand up on the gravel driveway right beside the car window. Much to Mr. Rigney's delight, he played several old songs and hymns, all of which were very familiar. They talked to each other as though they were longtime friends. Before we left, I took pictures, one of which was displayed on the wall of Mr. Rigney's apartment until his death.

Mr. Rigney with the accordion player.

On this and next page, Mr. Rigney listens intently to the accordion player.

Mr. Rigney with a former student, Greg Epperson, and Greg's mother Josephine, in Ararat, Virginia.

Josephine Epperson and Mr. Rigney.

Sara Leigh Collins with Mr. Rigney

Clarence Hall and his banjo.

Regular Visits with the Two Mr. Halls

While working at Patrick County High School, I came to know two teachers named Mr. Hall--Clarence Hall and Homer Hall--both of whom worked in the vocational department. These men looked nothing alike, but I had a terrible time remembering which one did which job. Homer Hall was an agriculture teacher, and Clarence Hall was the auto mechanics teacher. Both men were about the same age as Mr. Rigney, so they were all friends. We visited Clarence and Homer several times on our weekend rides.

During the first several visits to Clarence's home, we were blessed to meet and get to know his wife. Unfortunately, after a while, she unexpectedly died, leaving Mr. Hall very lonely and depressed. His health seemed to decline, and he became quite feeble.

He eventually had a stroke from which he did recover, but he had to make a few accommodations to his lifestyle. He could still drive to nearby locations such as church, doctors, and the grocery store. He was able to walk only with a walker, his talking was very low--difficult to hear and understand--and sadly, he lost control of his hand preventing him from playing his banjo, which was his favorite pastime.

When we visited after Mr. Hall's stroke, I would assist him to the car, where he would sit in the driver's seat and talk with Mr. Rigney. I could tell that hearing Mr. Hall was a task, but as he spoke, Mr. Rigney would lean in and try very hard to hear and understand what he said. One thing that always intrigued me was the fact that Mr. Rigney could indeed hear much of what Mr. Hall said to him even after he had the stroke.

It seemed that most of my communication with Mr. Rigney involved using my loudest possible speaking voice, bordering on yelling. Even then, he would often ask me to repeat what I had said. I think he had selective hearing, which was at its best when we visited his old friends. When the struggle to hear Mr. Hall became too difficult, Mr. Rigney would voluntarily say that we needed to leave.

Most of their conversations centered around Mr. Hall's health and his grief over his wife's death. They would also talk about the fact that Mr. Hall's days of publicly playing music were over, and he would re-live some of his musical experiences. Mr. Hall had also been an active square dancer, so that experience had also ended once his wife died.

I had purchased a walker tray for Mr. Rigney. This product had grooves that fit snuggly on each side of his walker, forming a little table for use when eating or writing. It also served as a good place to lay his newspaper while reading. Mr. Rigney wanted Mr. Hall to have one of these trays, so I ordered it from a Harriet Carter catalog.

When we went to deliver the tray, Mr. Hall was physically unable to come out to the car, so I stayed inside with him for a few minutes and reported back to Mr. Rigney.

While I was with him that day, he asked me if I would listen to a song he had written. It was a gospel song with beautiful lyrics about Christ. A friend of his had put it to music and recorded it. I loved his song, and he seemed to be at peace while sharing it with me. Mr. Hall was extremely proud of his masterpiece and asked me to tell Mr. Rigney about it. I knew Mr. Hall was an active local musician, but I did not know he was a song-writer too.

Clarence Hall has a daughter, but she lives in Florida, making it difficult for her to visit as much as he would have liked. He said she visited as often as she could, usually each month or so. Other than visits from neighbors, he spent much of his time alone. Mr. Rigney tried to make a point of checking on him every time we went to Stuart, so we saw him at least once, sometimes twice, each month.

As time went on, we were not finding him at home on Saturdays. I called friends of mine and inquired only to find out that he had needed some time in the local nursing/rehabilitation center while recovering from a surgical procedure.

Shortly after his recovery and return to his home, we found out that while helping another person clean a gun, which was another of his interests, he had been accidentally shot.

Thankfully it was not a fatal would, so Clarence would return to recover in the nursing home and eventually make it to the assisted living facility located beside the nursing home. Our visits with him concluded as Mr. Rigney was also becoming feebler and did not want to get in and out of the car to get inside the facility.

We also visited Homer Hall, the agricultural science teacher, several times. Homer had retired from PCHS and lived alone as his beautiful wife Margie had died of cancer many years ago.

At first, we had trouble finding Homer at home because he spent quite a bit of time with his adult children. The first time we visited Homer, he was still healthy and stayed in the front seat of the car with Mr. Rigney for well over an hour.

They talked about their years of working together at PCHS. Mr. Hall talked about his children and grandchildren and some of the health issues he had struggled with throughout the years.

Mr. Rigney told him about my son Rigney and gave him quite a few details about his amputations. As he often did, Mr. Rigney said, "Give me a nickel, and you can look at my leg." They both got a chuckle out this offer.

They spoke of students they had both taught, especially those living in the Ararat area. They also talked about the administrators they had worked for at PCHS. They had a great visit that beautiful Saturday. Mr. Hall also remembered me and tried to include me in their conversations, but as always, I didn't say much—I just let them talk.

The last time we visited Homer, we found him lying on his living room sofa looking very thin and frail. He had experienced quite a few health problems since our last visit, including a rough bout with pneumonia.

Homer's son, Patrick, was with him, and upon seeing me, Patrick asked, "Dad, do you remember Miss Honeycutt?" (my maiden name) Patrick had been a student at PCHS when I went to teach there, so that is the name he remembered. Mr. Hall did indeed remember me, and he knew why I was there. I asked Patrick if Homer was able to come to the car, and he helped him up and took him to my trusted front seat. They had a short conversation as Homer tired out very quickly. This would be the last time these two men saw each other.

Homer passed away about one year after Mr. Rigney's death.

Dr. Stewart Roberson with Mr. Rigney when they were visiting Dean Roberson at the Stuart, Virginia, hospital.

Mr. Rigney pictured with Dean Roberson during their final visit at her home in Stuart, Virginia.

Mr. Rigney and Dean Roberson

One summer day, Mr. Rigney wanted to visit his friend, Dean Roberson, who lived near Stuart Elementary School. I did not know this woman, nor did I have any idea which house was hers. We drove all over the area, and he pointed at the house he believed to be hers.

I went to the door, and a young man came out to talk to me. I realized immediately that this was not likely the right house because Mr. Rigney had told me that her children were around my age, which was the early fifties at that time. I asked him if he knew where she lived, and he said he didn't. I apologized for bothering him and continued my search.

I even went to a convenience store and tried to look up her address in a phone book. After riding around the area several times, Mr. Rigney finally pointed to a large yellow house on a hill and said, "That's her house. That's the one."

I drove up the hill to the house and knocked on the door, and sure enough, a well-dressed, beautiful, elderly lady with snow white hair greeted me. I introduced myself and told her my reason for being there. She was very enthusiastic about seeing Mr. Rigney as I assisted her down a steep outdoor stairway toward the front seat of the car.

I took my regular place in the back seat and listened as the two of them greeted each other and talked about their long ago days of teaching. He had, of course, taught both of her children. Mr. Rigney reminded her about her efforts to keep those boys in line. She bragged a bit about how her sons had turned out. He said, "They had no choice; they knew you would beat the hell out of them if they misbehaved." Mr. Rigney held her sons in the highest esteem, and I was very pleased when they both showed for his memorial service.

Ms. Roberson and Mr. Rigney fondly remembered school projects that they had worked on together many years before. She had assisted him with the one-act play troupe that he sponsored years ago at PCHS. She would sometimes go with him to the competitions since her son, Stewart, was an actor in the troupe. Mr. Rigney could claim the first ever state championships for the new Patrick County High School by producing three consecutive One-Act play state champions between 1971 and 1973.

I think she may have been the most entertaining of all of the friends we visited. I chuckled when he looked at her fashionably painted fingernails and asked, "Why do you paint your fingernails?" and she replied that she just enjoyed having her nails look nice.

He then followed up with, "Well, do you paint your toenails too?" She told him she certainly did and stuck her foot out for him to see. He then offered to let her look at his leg for a nickel, and they laughed.

Mr. Rigney chastised her because she had remarried after her first husband died. He said, "You knew that I was available," and she responded, "George, I didn't know you were interested."

They both laughed and remembered what good friends they had been when they were young. The two of them never dated each other as she was already married when he came to Patrick County, but they surely flirted as though they had.

Because the two of them enjoyed each other's company so much, we had several similar visits with Mrs. Roberson in the months to come. One particular Sunday afternoon, we went to visit her at her house, and she was not there. Her car was in the driveway, and her beautifully decorated porch was still covered with green ferns and colorful plants. Everything seemed to be in its place, but we couldn't find her.

We saw some neighbors in their yard and stopped to inquire only to learn that Mrs. Roberson had taken a serious fall and had been in the hospital for several weeks. We immediately drove to the hospital, where I was given instructions by Mr. Rigney to go in and check on her.

After inquiring about the location of her room, I found it at the end of a very long hallway. She smiled brightly when I entered, but didn't really seem to know who I was. As was often the case with Mr. Rigney's friends, I had to re-introduce myself to her.

Once I mentioned Mr. Rigney, she immediately knew who I was. I explained that he was not able to come in, which was not altogether true. He was physically able to come inside, but he refused to allow her to see him in a wheelchair, so he stayed in the car. He declared that there was no way he would allow her to see him "parked up in a damned wheelchair."

She told me that her son, Stewart, was visiting, but had just stepped out and would return momentarily. She was sure he would want to see Mr. Rigney. She was right.

When Stewart returned, I walked him to the car where a very surprised Mr. Rigney delightfully greeted him with his typical "How ya doin?'" Stewart's time with him would become ingrained in Mr. Rigney's memory until the day he died.

He bragged about Stewart frequently because he had been named Virginia's State Superintendent of the Year. He was one of Mr. Rigney's prized students. I took pictures of them and, of course, they were displayed on the wall of his apartment until he died.

I then returned to the hospital room to visit with Mrs. Roberson while they finished their visit in the car. I learned from her that she had fallen and seriously broke her collarbone. She was very weak and unable to move around at all, but her white hair was perfectly in place. Despite everything, she looked beautiful. She was spending most of her days confined to bed, having been through surgeries and continuing therapies.

When I got back to the car, Stewart confirmed that she would be in the hospital for quite a while, and he was concerned about her future as her memory was also failing her. That was evident when she would see me enter her room, but she always remembered Mr. Rigney, and she was always quite lucid and accurate during their conversations. He never even realized that she had a memory problem, but he did say that she lied to him about her age. I don't if she did or not. She had told him she was 82. At this writing, she is 93.

Upon our next visit, Mr. Rigney decided he would go inside and visit. He had planned to use his walker to make his way down the extremely long hallway leading to her room. I was filled with dread because I knew that his slow walking pace would require hours to reach her room. I was able to get him out of the car at the ramp without incident, and I got him inside the hospital doors. I told him to wait for me there while I parked the car in a proper parking space.

He was patiently waiting for me when I went back inside the hospital. As we started down the hallway using his walker, I offered to get a hospital wheelchair to make this walk more expedient.

At first, he would hear nothing of this, but as we started the walk, and he saw how long the hallway was, he said, "Go ahead and get me that wheelchair."

I was so thankful because I was worried about getting him to Mrs. Roberson's room.

He said, "She probably won't care if I'm in a wheelchair."

I pointed out to him that she couldn't walk either, so she likely would think nothing of it. She didn't. She was unbelievably excited to see him.

He kept jokingly asking her, "Who "beat the hell out of you?"

She responded, "Oh, I don't know who she was."

They would continue this type of jovial bantering for at least an hour. I was fortunate enough to find a local newspaper to read while they visited.

Once he saw how simple it was to transfer to a wheelchair and get to her room, we would have several such visits with Mrs. Roberson while she was in the hospital. Future visits required the purchase of a gift, which I would usually find at the local Rite-Aid. He usually wanted to give her candy or cookies, but one day we took her a puzzle, and we often took cards.

One of our visits happened to fall on Valentine's Day. I went to Rite-Aid and bought her Ghirardelli chocolates. She was delighted to get candy but would have been happy just to see him. They once again visited while I read the local paper. Even though her memory was failing, she always thanked me and showed great appreciation to me for bringing him to see her.

Mrs. Roberson was eventually released from the hospital to live at the assisted living complex located near the hospital. We had not planned to see her there, so he wrote her a letter to which he did not receive a reply.

He couldn't stand not having a reply, so one day as I was driving him around, he decided he wanted to visit her in the memory care unit. I went inside and asked one of the attendants if she would allow Mrs. Roberson to come outside and visit with him. While I got Mr. Rigney out of the car, the nurse brought Mrs. Roberson out so that they could sit together for a short while in the heat of the summer day.

I could tell her memory was getting worse when I spoke to her, but I found it interesting how lucid she was while engaging in conversation with him. They did, of course, always talk about the same topics, which included Stewart being Superintendent of the Year several years earlier, Chip, her other son, and my son, Rigney. They would always speak about their days as teachers during these conversations. Perhaps it was the repetition that made conversing so effortless for them.

He, of course, asked her if she received his card and letter, but she didn't seem to know what he was talking about. We never knew for sure if she received it.

That would be the last time the two of them saw each other. It was less than three months later that Mr. Rigney passed away. I'm so thankful they had this little time together.

Radford University

One rainy Saturday morning, I arrived for my visit with Mr. Rigney. He knew we would not be able to go out that day because of the weather, but he was still very excited.

"Look what I found at the thrift store," he announced as he held up a copy of a Radford University yearbook from the early 1960s.

He had placed markers throughout the book, so he could easily locate pictures of his professors. While none of these were familiar to me, he acted as though I should know all of them personally.

He would point to each person of interest and give me a detailed description of the person and how they came to be a part of his life. I had heard him speak of Dr. Martin as he was the professor who encouraged him to study special education, but all I knew about him were the things Mr. Rigney had told me. He used this yearbook to ensure that I would be able to place a face with the professors he spoke of so often.

He had not seen most of these people in over fifty years, and the majority of them had been dead for some time. They remained very real to Mr. Rigney, and he wanted to share these experiences with me. He gave me a description of each one he remembered and shared an experience.

**George Rigney's graduation portrait when
he earned his bachelor's degree in 1962.**

When I learned that he got this yearbook at a thrift store, I asked him how he came to find it among the many books lining the back wall. He explained that on his way out of the store, he passed by a trashcan and saw the yearbook, which was about to be thrown away. He took it from the trash can and spent many days perusing the pictures and remembering his younger days.

"I just don't understand why they would have tried to throw out something like this. It is the most valuable thing in the store."

Mr. Rigney was incredibly proud of his Alma Mater. He had always treasured the degrees that he earned at Radford College, so he considered it a great loss when they burned in his house fire. During his hospital stays, he repeatedly mentioned that he was no longer a "degreed man." Hearing these words distressed me, so I went through the process of getting replacement degrees for him. When they arrived, I had them framed, and his niece placed them on his wall beside other accolades he had earned through the years.

These degrees are currently on display in the home of a nephew that I never knew. I am happy they are in a safe location.

Another related item that Mr. Rigney no longer had possession of was his Radford College class ring. He told me he wished he could get it back, but "it is gone forever."

I asked him what happened to it, thinking that maybe I could ask Brenda Kaye to find it for him.

He said, "It was pawned a long time ago." His great-nephew, who had fallen on hard financial times, needed money, and "he asked me if he could sell the ring for money. He took it to a pawn shop and sold it. Oh, it doesn't matter anymore; it was just an ole ring."

For Christmas 2014, Rigney, my son, and I ordered him a new class ring almost identical to the description he had previously given of the original ring. Rigney and his wife, Jessalyn, took the ring to him a couple of days before Christmas.

Rigney reported, "He examined every angle of the ring, commenting on how it was exactly like the first one. I don't think I have ever seen him so excited."

He realized it was a new ring, as opposed to his original ring, but he couldn't understand how we had gotten a replica of his. He was not only excited but humbled that we had managed to get one almost exactly like his without having ever seen it. I must admit some of that was pure luck. I knew the color of the stone, and I took a chance on choosing white gold. I then selected a large RU for one side and the education symbol for the other.

We had been worried about the size, but I made an educated estimate of 10.5 when we placed the order. The ring was a very tight fit on the right-hand ring finger, but a perfect fit on the left hand. Rigney told him we could either send it back or take it to a jeweler to be more adequately sized. He refused to let go of it even long enough to have it resized.

He said, "It's a perfect fit on this finger, and I will be wearing it all the time."

True to his word, he did wear it all the time except at night. He put it back in the case and placed it in a drawer on his nightstand for safekeeping. He did this daily for a while and then decided that "someone might come in and try to steal it." After making this realization, he wore the ring all the time.

When we visited friends, he would stick his hand out and say, "Look what my boy gave me for Christmas."

I'm pretty sure he thought the ring was the best gift he ever received. He would wear it to his grave in 2018.

I often asked Mr. Rigney to let me drive him to Radford University so that he could see it one last time.

He would always come up with some excuse not to go, usually saying, "No, that's just too far. No need to go back up there; it's been too long." I never pressed the issue as I usually allowed him to choose where we went.

I visited Mr. Rigney on a beautiful Saturday morning right before Christmas in 2015, and he didn't want to visit friends because he suspected they might be involved in Christmas activities.

Knowing he was probably right, I suggested that we just go for a ride and come back home. I drove him to Foster Falls, a small, historic, mostly deserted town, along the New River. We both loved that place and had been there together several times before.

We went there together with my son when he was three years old. That was a favorite memory for Mr. Rigney as he would often describe every minute detail of that little day trip. As we rode by the river, he recalled how Rigney "had wanted to jump in the water when he was three years old." He had scared Mr. Rigney because he didn't realize that Rigney was already an active swimmer. All he did that day was take off his shoes and wade, but Mr. Rigney remembered it forever.

There was nothing to do there except look at the beautiful scenic views of mountainous pastureland and the New River, so our visit was short.

As we left, I saw a sign for Interstate-81 just a few miles ahead. Without saying a word, I drove a few miles in that direction and got on I-81 toward Radford, Virginia. I didn't say a word about where we were going. We were probably about an hour's drive away from the university, but he never asked where we were going.

As we approached the exit sign for Radford University, I asked, "Do you know where we are?"

He replied, "Do you think I wouldn't recognize Radford University? I spent ten summers of my life up here."

As we drove toward the university, he would point at various buildings and say, "It's all different. That building was not here. It must've been built after I left."

I was determined to find a part of campus that would be at least vaguely familiar to him. He finally saw a building with a large clock tower that he recognized as a place where he had had various experiences as a graduate student. There was a parking space in front of it, so I parked the car and asked him if he wanted to get out of the car. He said that he could see the buildings from his seat in the car.

I got out of the car and took pictures of that building while he looked around at other buildings that he started to recognize.

He suddenly spoke very excitedly, "There it is. There's McGuffey Training School."

He was correct, but the building is now called Whitt Hall as the name had been changed.

Our time at Radford University that day was short, but we slowly drove throughout the campus, allowing him his final opportunity to go back in time as much as possible and remember his days as a student. He enjoyed looking at the very old buildings as he came to recognize them.

As we drove back home, he told me a story about a classmate whose name I cannot recall. Mr. Rigney told me there had been a newspaper article about the man's lucrative career in education in one of the Virginia newspapers recently. Strangely, there had been no mention of his ever having attended Radford University.

"I had just passed my final comprehensive examination and was ready to graduate. I saw him as I was going to pick up my graduation gown. I told him to come with me, and we would pick them up together.

He said, 'George, I won't be graduating. I didn't pass the final comprehensive exam.'"

He went on to explain to me that the man was African-American, and no person of color had ever earned a degree from Radford College at that time. While waiting outside the room where his comprehensive examinations were scheduled to take place, Mr. Rigney had overheard a conversation between two university officials.

Mr. Rigney said, "I told him to come with me, but I didn't tell him where we were going."

He was a bit confused about where they were going and why, but the young man accompanied Mr. Rigney to the office of the college president, and they managed to speak with him. Mr. Rigney told the president that he had overheard two school employees discussing whether the college was culturally ready to issue a degree to a black man. Mr. Rigney voiced his opinion about the unfairness of this decision and requested that the student receive a second opportunity to complete the comprehensive exam in front of a different panel.

After making his compelling argument, the young black student was granted a second chance and graduated as the first African-American to ever receive a degree from Radford College. He would go on to serve as an educational advisor to various government officials.

After the news article appeared, I used the internet to track down a phone number for the man. I finally was able to reach him by phone, and he confirmed that he was the first African American ever to receive a degree from Radford.

When I asked him about Mr. Rigney, he said, "His name sounds familiar."

Our trip to Radford University would be a subject that he talked about until he died. I offered to take him back a few times, but he said the one trip was enough. That was a beautiful day, and I will be forever grateful that he got to see his beloved Alma Mater one last time.

Pictured is Whitt Hall at Radford University. When Mr. Rigney was a student, the building was the McGuffy Teacher Training School.

Mr. Rigney sports his Radford University jacket that Rigney Marcela gave him for Christmas the December he visited Radford University for the final time.

Mr. Rigney visiting Melinda Comer, a retired special education teacher and graduate of Radford University.

Marvin Foley

I had never heard the name Marvin Foley before Mr. Rigney informed me that we would be visiting him. I would learn that he lived in a white house on a hill on Shingle Shop Road in Stuart. Although I had driven by that road many, many times, I had never paid attention to its name. Given that Mr. Rigney had a talent for remembering road and community names, I followed his directions and arrived at Marvin's house without incident.

There was a huge workshop behind the house, so we drove back there, expecting to find Marvin. I got out of the car and asked, "Are you Marvin Foley?" He answered, "Who wants to know?" and I said, "George Rigney." He dropped whatever he was working on and made his way to the passenger window of the car, where he stood for the next hour or so.

Mr. Foley was a big, burly man, probably a few years younger than Mr. Rigney. He had a great sense of humor, so they exchanged jokes and laughter for the duration of our visit.

I would learn that Mr. Foley had once been a school principal. The two of them talked at length about their days of working together, but it seems that Mr. Foley just wanted to take his career in a different direction. He started his own business erecting aluminum buildings in various parts of Virginia and surrounding states.

Like Mr. Rigney, Mr. Foley loved nature. He built birdbaths on his property and enjoyed watching the birds fly in and out. Mr. Foley grew beautiful vegetable gardens. One day, he asked me if I would like to have some green beans and squash. Thinking that he had them ready to give to me, I said, "Sure." He handed me a plastic bag and told me to pick all I wanted. I don't enjoy gardening, and I surely don't enjoy picking green beans, but I picked a bagful, along with a second bag of squash.

After we paid Mr. Foley our first visit, he returned the favor by surprising Mr. Rigney with a visit at his apartment. He was in the Hillsville area on a work project, so he was driving one of his big work trucks. He asked Mr. Rigney to go out for a ride with him. I have no idea how the two of them managed to get Mr. Rigney into that big truck. I am glad this happened without my knowledge, as I would have been extremely worried about a possible disaster. I'm not even sure where they went, but I know that visit surely meant a lot to Mr. Rigney.

We reciprocated with another visit to Mr. Foley's house a few months later on a cold, beautiful day in January. I was driving my husband's Jeep because the weather and travel conditions are sometimes unpredictable at that time of year. Since it was cold, this visit would take place with Mr. Foley sitting in the driver's seat with me in the back.

Suddenly, Mr. Foley cranked my Jeep and said, "George, I want to show you my property on the other side of the road." I found it a bit unnerving that he just started up my Jeep and took off driving, but I figured I had no cause to worry. He expertly navigated the jeep through the rolling fields, occasionally stopping to point out various areas of interest. Eventually, he would turn around and drive us back to his house. We concluded our visit with plans to return when the weather got warmer. We did return several times before Mr. Rigney's death.

As we were planning Mr. Rigney's memorial service, Phyllis Eastridge called Mr. Foley to ask him if he would like to speak. I was somewhat disappointed when I received a message that he was having back problems and would be unable to attend the service, but I understood.

He did call me a few weeks after the service to offer his condolences and to let me know that he had prepared a brief eulogy that he had intended to deliver. He thanked me profusely for the many times I had driven Mr. Rigney to visit him.

In mid-December 2018, I received a Christmas card from Mr. Foley. He had written me a very nice note and enclosed a generous check that would go toward the scholarship fund.

With both my boys being with their significant others on Christmas Eve and my husband being out on a work assignment, I found myself at home alone for a few hours. I decided to call Mr. Foley and thank him for the donation. I was worried that he might be engaged in a family event, given that it was Christmas Eve, but he was alone and very happy to hear from me. He praised my relationship with Mr. Rigney and further explained how pleased he was that they were able to reconnect during those few years.

Mr. Foley was a true friend to Mr. Rigney and became a friend to me too. We still have an occasional phone conversation just to catch up and talk about Mr. Rigney.

The Infection

While at work one day, I received a call from Brenda Kaye. She was informing me that Mr. Rigney had a bloody open spot on the top of his foot. She believed it was infected, and he should see a doctor. Brenda said he had been keeping it a secret from everyone except her. She had been cleaning and bandaging it for some time.

I had initially thought it might have been a delayed problem with the skin grafts he had in 2012 because her description placed the wound below the grafts. I remembered there had been a spot that was slow to heal, causing his surgeons to keep a close eye on it before they released him from medical treatment.

My first instinct was to call his surgeons and make an appointment. After speaking to various phone operators and receptionists at Wake Forest Medical Center, I was finally transferred to the right office. They were willing to make an appointment for the surgeon to see him, but he told his niece he wanted no part of that. I kind of understood because he knew the wound was serious enough that he would run the risk of a return to the hospital or nursing home.

Since I was two hours away from him, I didn't know what to do. I decided to call Dr. Rick Cole, who was not only a former student but his attending physician at the nursing center during his recovery from the amputations. The receptionist offered an appointment two weeks later. I tried to explain that he shouldn't wait that long, so I asked that my call be transferred to a nurse.

I described the situation to the nurse, and like the receptionist, she said they had no appointments to offer as Dr. Cole would be leaving town for several days. I asked her if she would tell Dr. Cole that his former teacher, Mr. Rigney, needed an immediate appointment. I was on hold for a short while when she returned to tell me that Dr. Cole would see him the next morning at 8:30 AM. I have no idea what their conversation entailed, but I was not at all surprised that Dr. Cole was willing to take the time to see him,

Given that it was afternoon when the nurse made the appointment, I had much to do to prepare to leave the next morning. To get to his home, I would need to travel for two hours, pick him up, and travel another hour to reach the doctor's office. That meant I would be leaving my Boone home at 5:30 AM the next morning. I had to acquire a substitute teacher and prepare lesson plans as I would be taking the day off.

I decided to call Brenda Kaye and ask her to tell him that he had the appointment with Dr. Cole, and I would arrive to pick him up around 7:15 the next morning. I knew if he didn't know that I was coming, he would not be out of the bed.

She did as I asked, but he told her there was no way he was seeing any doctor. I knew, based on Brenda Kaye's description, his hesitancy was because his wound was bad enough that most any doctor would put him in the hospital, which again might have led to a nursing home placement. I also knew the seriousness of the problem because Brenda Kay would not have called if she had any other option. Unfortunately, neither she nor I had his Medical Power of Attorney and really could not force the issue.

Given his resistance to the doctor, I told Brenda Kay to let him know that I would be coming up on Saturday, and I wanted to see the wound. He was prepared to show it to me when I arrived. It was a bloody red area about the size of a quarter located on top of the foot just below the skin grafted area. There was a small amount of pus oozing around the edges. The area was not scabbed over; it was just a raw, bloody mess. He insisted that the problem arose from the insert inside his shoe. I think he may have been right, but since he refused to go to the doctor or his prosthetist, we would never know.

I prepared a basin of water, and he soaked the wound. I put antibiotic cream on it and bandaged it up myself. I then went to the pharmacy and described the situation to a pharmacist who encouraged me to get him to the doctor. After telling him that a doctor was not a possibility, he showed me the best bandages and medications for treatment.

It became my routine job to clean and bandage his wound, so I researched the problem. While I have no medical knowledge or training, the best I could determine was that he had a foot ulcer. I found similar pictures on the internet and remembered that my aunt had a similar spot on her ankle.

My sister, who had taken care of my aunt, told me to use raw honey on the wound after thoroughly cleaning it. I followed her instructions, but since I lived so far from him, and could only make the trip every other week, there was little healing. The good news was that it didn't get any worse for quite a while.

Treating his wound became routine for about a year. I was always hopeful that I would pull the bandage off to find some semblance of healing, but it didn't happen. I was able to put a heavy sock over his bandage and then a soft shoe if he needed to walk.

Because Mr. Rigney could not step down from the sidewalk to the ground in front of his room, he had to walk at least one hundred feet to reach a level area where he was physically able to get into the car. He had said that walking caused his foot to hurt terribly, so we stopped our weekend travels for almost a year.

One day I arrived to find that the facility owners had conveniently, without his request, built a ramp very close to his door. I think the ramp may have been built to accommodate another tenant, but it surely made traveling accessible because his walk was probably no more than twenty feet. I was able to resume taking him out for weekend rides.

Once this ramp was built, we were back on the road again. I worried every time I saw the wound realizing that it was not healing, but if he wanted to go out, and I could get him down the ramp, we went. I am so glad we did because it would only be less than one year later that Mr. Rigney died.

The door to Mr. Rigney's apartment shown above and below, the newly constructed ramp in front of his room.

Visits to Rigney's Home

In December 2016, my son, Rigney, graduated from Western Carolina University with a bachelor's degree in Elementary Education and Special Education. While he was not in attendance, that was a proud day for Mr. Rigney. He felt like Rigney was following in his footsteps.

While at Western Carolina, not only had Rigney earned a degree, but he had also met Jessalyn Jenks, the girl of his dreams. Mr. Rigney had met Jessalyn and declared her the "most beautiful woman to ever walk through the door." It came as no surprise to us that Rigney proposed to her the weekend following his graduation.

To make matters even better, Rigney was fortunate enough to land a job at JV Washam Elementary School in Cornelius, North Carolina, very close to the neighborhood where he had grown up. He rented an apartment close to his school in the Lake Norman area in the suburbs of Charlotte, North Carolina.

In June 2017, shortly after school was out for the year, I went to Hillsville and picked up Mr. Rigney for a ride. I asked him if he would like to visit Rigney at his apartment in Cornelius.

He excitedly said, "Oh, I don't know. That is a long way for you to drive."

I had expected him to react similarly, so I said, "Well, let's just get in the car, and we will figure it out."

Neither of us said another word about where we were going. I drove a few miles on Highway 52 South, picked up Interstate 77 South, and kept on driving until I reached Exit 28 in Cornelius. We drove into the parking lot of Rigney's apartment just as he was arriving home from a day of teaching tennis lessons at one of the local country clubs.

They were both incredibly excited to see each other. Mr. Rigney sat in the car while Rigney stood next to him at the passenger side window. I left them alone for a while and took Rigney's dog, Howie, for a walk. I didn't hear very much of their conversation, but it didn't take a genius to figure out that they were talking about Rigney's first semester of teaching.

As we prepared to leave, Mr. Rigney said, "Well, I feel like you should be leaving with us." Rigney told him he better stay there as Jessalyn was coming for a visit when she got off work.

When we left, I drove past the elementary school where Rigney teaches. We then drove to William Amos Hough High School, where Rigney had graduated, and I had taught for two years. We then proceeded to North Mecklenburg High School, where my oldest son Braxton had graduated, and where I had taught for four years. We then looped around to the western side of Huntersville and drove by Longcreek Elementary School, where Rigney had attended fifth grade the year we moved. We continued north on Beatties Ford Road past Francis Bradley Middle School, where both boys had attended, and I had taught for two years.

After looking at all of the schools, I proceeded through suburban Friday afternoon traffic back to Interstate 77-North. We were approximately one hundred miles from Hillsville, so we had a long journey.

As we traveled along the interstate, Mr. Rigney repeated, "I feel like my boy should be coming home with us. It seems strange to leave him in that big city all by himself."

I explained, "Rigney is now a big boy with a teaching job and a fiancée.' He doesn't need to come home with us."

"Well, I just don't know how he grew up so fast." He then referenced the day he and I took Rigney to Foster Falls and continued to repeat that "it just didn't seem right to leave him there all by himself."

These comments did not stop at the end of our trip, but he would repeat them numerous times when I visited him in the future.

A year passed before I would mention visiting Rigney again. By then, he and Jessalyn had married and bought a house located less than a mile from the school where he teaches. I had called ahead and asked Brenda Kaye to tell him we were going to visit Rigney and Jessalyn in their new home.

She called me back and said he didn't want to go that far from home again. I said, "That's okay. We will go somewhere else."

I had just bought a brand new Honda CRV and drove to Hillsville to take him for his first ride in it. By this point, we had completely worn out my father-in-law's Mercury Grand Marquis. I sold it to my mechanic for two hundred dollars.

When I arrived at this apartment, I said, "You can decide where you want to go. We won't go see Rigney if you don't want to."

He looked at me and said, "So you don't want to go see my boy. I thought we were going to see my boy."

"I would love to go see Rigney, but you told Brenda Kaye you didn't want to go."

He didn't say another word. He put on his hat and used his walker to pull up from his wheelchair. We made our way to the ramp so that he could get into my new car. He stopped on his way and said, "Why did you buy an ugly car?"

I laughed and said, "Mr. Rigney, just get in the car."

We made the long trip to Cornelius once again. It was an incredibly hot day on the mountain, so I knew it would be much hotter as we drew near to Charlotte. We stopped along the way to fill up with gas, and we bought a huge cantaloupe to take to them.

We called ahead and let them know we were coming. When we arrived, they came out of the house to visit with us. After saying our hellos, Jessalyn and I went inside the house where it was cool. Rigney got into the driver's seat and took Mr. Rigney for a ride through his neighborhood and out to his school. He was able to drive him to the door of his mobile classroom.

After a while, they returned, and it was time for us to start our journey back to Hillsville. Contrary to what he had repeated after our previous visit, he said, "I don't feel bad leaving him this time. He has his own home and a wife. I didn't like leaving him by himself last time, but now it is different."

He continuously made similar statements all the way home. I am so thankful I took him to see Rigney content in his new home with his new bride. It would be only three months later that he died.

Jessalyn Marcela is shown with Mr. Rigney in his apartment in Hillsville.

Final Visits

On August 25, 2018, I arrived as usual for a Saturday morning out with Mr. Rigney. He was eager to leave his room, but he had not prepared well as his clothes were not fresh, and he didn't seem very strong. I managed to get him in the car with little incident. He was even reluctant to tell me where he wanted to go or whom he wished to see. I asked him if he wanted to travel on Highway 52 North or South. We opted to go south down the mountain toward Mount Airy. I told him he could decide where we were going as we traveled.

We made our regular stop for gas in Cana, Virginia. Mr. Rigney was very fond of the young man who pumped our gas there on Saturdays. He was probably about thirty years old, wore cargo shorts and t-shirts, and sported a long brown ponytail. Mr. Rigney was always adamant that we give this man a tip once he pumped our gas. Although we never learned this gentleman's name, he too had become a fixture in our regular Saturday morning rides.

After getting our gas, we proceeded on toward Mount Airy, stopping by McDonald's drive-thru to pick up some lunch for me to eat on our way to wherever we were going. By the time we finished at the drive-thru with a small hamburger and large iced tea, Mr. Rigney had decided we would be visiting Mack George, a former guidance counselor at Patrick County High School, who lived in Stokes County just inside the North Carolina/Virginia border east of Mount Airy.

We had been to Mr. George's house before, so I knew it was located far out in rural Stokes County, at least an hour's drive from where we were. As we traveled, Mr. Rigney talked relentlessly about what a great guidance counselor Mr. George had been. I already knew what a great counselor he had been because I had also worked with Mr. George. Mr. George and Mr. Rigney worked together to formulate plans and schedules that would allow the graduation of boys who might never have even considered finishing high school. Both of these men went to bat for students who had no one else in their corner.

When we finally arrived at the George homeplace, I went to the door and spoke with Brian, Mr. George's son. He, too, was quite a character. I informed him that George Rigney was in my car, and he seemed as delighted as his father. They were actually in the middle of eating lunch, but they dropped everything and came out to visit.

Like Mr. Rigney, Mr. George was a small man in size, but his character surely made him seem large. He was also quite a jokester. He and Mr. Rigney bantered back and forth with each other for over an hour.

Mr. Rigney said, "I'll show you my leg for a nickel," a phrase he loved to say to anyone who knew or maybe didn't know about his prosthetic leg.

Mr. George would reply with some humorous comment relating to his own mobility issues as he had broken his leg a few months before our visit. Sometimes, Brian would chime in with some humor of his own. I sat quietly unless one of them addressed me as I didn't see a need to disturb the three of them.

They would also talk about their experiences at PCHS, even citing names of specific students whom they helped to make it through high school. Together, they had managed to help some of these students get vocational scholarships at Patrick Henry Community College or Wythe Community College, allowing them to develop career paths that led to great success.

This visit ended in the early afternoon, so Mr. Rigney decided he wanted to see Bruce Dollarhite, a retired electronics teacher at PCHS. He lived about another forty-five minutes from Mr. George, but we had time.

We had visited Mr. Dollarhite on numerous other occasions and had always been welcomed by both him and his wife. Mr. Dollarhite was one of Mr. Rigney's favorite people, and I, too, came to admire him.

Mr. Dollarhite stood over six feet tall and was the epitome of a southern gentleman. He was extremely welcoming and patient during Mr. Rigney's visits. He had bought the local radio station after his retirement from teaching, so he was well known and respected in the community.

On this particular Saturday, Mr. and Mrs. Dollarhite were entertaining their grandchildren. They were at their dining room table, enjoying takeout food from one of the local fast food restaurants. I surely hated interrupting them, and seeing that they were eating, I told them we could come back another day. Like Mr. George had done a little earlier, Mr. Dollarhite rose from his chair, wrapped his lunch, and went to the car, where he visited with Mr. Rigney for about an hour.

I don't know what they talked about as Mrs. Dollarhite invited me to stay inside. After a very pleasant visit with her and her grandchildren, I went back to the car as the afternoon was quickly moving along.

The two men seemed to have had a pleasant conversation and exchanged good-byes. They had no way of knowing this would be the last time Mr. Rigney would come to the Dollarhite home.

Mr. Rigney talked about Mr. Dollarhite and Mr. George almost all the way home. He repeatedly said, "Bruce Dollarhite is the finest...the finest" or "They don't make 'em like Mack George anymore." Given my experience with both these men, I was inclined to agree with him.

None of these three men had any way of knowing that this would be their last visit, but I don't think that Saturday could have been any better. While this was not the last time, I would take Mr. Rigney out for Saturday visits. This was the last visit with these two gentlemen.

Mr. Rigney's good friend and colleague, Mack George.

**Fred Brim and Mrs. Jennifer Cox, Principal of Blue Ridge
Elementary School.**

Our Last Ride

Karen Kingsbury, a popular writer of Christian novels, wrote a poem entitled "Let Me Hold You Longer," in which she laments about "last" events with her children. The theme of her poem is a mother remembering her child's many milestones while growing up and preparing to move away. She concludes her poem by asking, "Let me hold on longer, God, to every precious last." One of the "lasts" she notes is, "The last time that you need me for a ride from here to there." While I was not Mr. Rigney's caregiver, nor was he a child, those lines remind me of the last ride I took with Mr. Rigney on September 1, 2018, before his death on September 30, 2018.

If I could have possibly known it was our last ride together, the only thing I would have done differently was appreciate it more at the time. That's all I could have done differently because I did everything he asked me to do that day.

It was a beautiful coming of a fall day with "ideal" weather, as he repeatedly noted throughout the day. That was the time of year that he loved the most because it was not hot, nor was it yet cold. After picking him up at his apartment, we drove to Ararat, Virginia, to check on Ray Smith, the retired social studies teacher, and friend. We had visited Ray numerous times as he was one of Mr. Rigney's closest friends at Patrick County High School. Ray was always happy to visit with Mr. Rigney, and as many did, sat in the driver's seat while I sat in the back, usually for long periods of time.

This particular visit was different because Ray was visibly upset and in a hurry, as he was about to leave for the pharmacy while his son was available to sit with Mrs. Smith, who was extremely ill and, unbeknownst to us, expected to die within a few days. Although this short visit was quite sorrowful, Mr. Rigney had the opportunity to offer condolences and peace to this family who was about to face the death of someone they loved.

Mr. Rigney's presence, even for this short amount of time, seemed to bring comfort to Ray in this time of sorrow. During our departure, he repeatedly thanked us and told us how glad he was to see us even if he couldn't take time to talk.

Mr. Rigney never knew that Mrs. Smith died a few hours after we left. I didn't find out myself until I saw Ray at Mr. Rigney's memorial service two months later.

Our next stop that day was the home of Fred and Alice Brim. Mr. Brim had been the assistant principal of Patrick County High School while both Mr. Rigney and I worked there. He was such a wonderful man and a dear friend to both of us, and he was delighted to see us as always.

Although Mr. Brim had some health problems of his own, he managed to get to the driver's seat of the car for a very long visit. While they visited, I went into the house with Alice, so I don't know much about their conversation that day. However, this was not the first time we had visited the Brims, so I had heard the two of them talk about their many years of friendship and working together in the schools. Usually, their biggest topic of conversation was how schools had changed throughout their years of educational experiences.

Their days of working together went back many, many years. Mr. Brim had been single when the two of them started working together. He now had grown children, both of whom Mr. Rigney knew at Patrick County High School. They knew many of the same people, and they referred to each other as "school men."

After an hour or so into the visit, Mrs. Brim and I thought we should go out and bring her husband back into the house, given that he had health problems and should probably rest in a more comfortable setting. We both went out, but neither of them were ready for the visit to stop. They continued to talk for quite a while before the visit concluded. On this particular day, they both seemed reluctant to let go of each other, but one of the final things that Mr. Rigney said to Mr. Brim was, "When spring comes, and we feel better, I will be back. We will get out of the car and sit at the table on your porch." They parted ways for the final time with that thought.

When I called Mr. Brim to tell him that Mr. Rigney had passed away, he relayed those words to me with comfort. With both Mr. Brim and Mr. Rigney approaching their late-eighties, they still made plans to see each other again. While that is no longer possible on this earth, Mr. Brim later assured me that it would happen in a better place.

After leaving the Brims, we started back toward home as evening was approaching. Although Mr. Rigney was happy and talkative, I knew that he was extremely tired and needed to go home. I had a very difficult time getting him out of the car. I became extremely worried and was feeling a bit helpless as I tried to help him gain his balance.

He managed to get his walker onto the ramp, and he slowly started the short (but long for him) journey up the small ramp. Once he got to the top of the ramp, he had about six more feet to get to his door. I was very thankful when I got him inside and seated in his wheelchair by the window.

I went back outside to move my car to a parking space and out of the way of the other tenants. I was so exhausted that I sat in the car for just a few seconds, and thoughts passed through my mind that I wish I could erase. I wondered how much longer I could keep getting him in and out of the house by myself. I wondered if I was even doing the right thing by taking him out, knowing that his foot was so infected. I made a conscious decision that I was going to do it as long as he said he was able whether I thought he was or not. I also concluded that I hoped that would be a long time, so I would just have to keep up my strength and do what I had to do.

I went back in his apartment and proceeded to change his bedsheets and clean the floor as best I could. I then prepared water for him to soak his foot, so I could treat it and bandage it. There was no healing of his foot, and I noticed an unpleasant odor emitting from it, similar to the infectious odor following his frostbite. I was very worried that he was developing gangrene as he had before his amputations. I asked him again about calling Dr. Cole, but he refused to allow it. I treated his ulcer with raw honey, bandaged it up, and after making sure he had everything he needed, I left.

I had no way of knowing that I would never return to his apartment again. I did not know that would be the last time he "would need me for a ride from here to there." If I had, I might have asked God to "let me hold on a little longer."

Mr. Rigney's Death

I am not sure I have, or if I ever will be, completely adjusted to his death as I miss him every day. On September 30, 2018, Mr. Rigney went on to heaven.

I had planned to spend Saturday, September 15, with him, but there was a hurricane moving along the North Carolina coastline, causing strong winds and heavy rain even in our mountainous area. He had asked Brenda Kaye to call and make sure I "had sense enough to stay at home during a hurricane." I told her to tell him that I would wait until the following Saturday to come.

Since the hurricane had not yet caused serious problems on Saturday morning, I considered going to see him anyway, but it began to rain. I was afraid travel conditions would quickly worsen, making my return to Boone difficult.

Little did I know that he would take ill and be transported to the hospital in Galax, Virginia, on September 17, 2018. I did not find out until two days later, after he was transferred to Forsyth Hospital in Winston-Salem, NC.

I don't know why his family chose not to let me know of his hospitalization, but a friend of his niece called me on Wednesday, giving me as much information as she had. I immediately left for the hospital, which was two hours away. The lady who called reported that doctors had told the family that his body was full of infection--no doubt a result of the ulcer on his foot. This infection was too serious to treat at the local hospital in Galax, prompting the transfer to Forsyth.

He was immediately given strong antibiotics, which seemed to be working to fight the infection. However, upon further testing, his doctors believed that he had a mild heart attack. The cardiologist also reported that blood was not pumping properly to his heart. I was with him when the cardiologist tried to explain the seriousness of his condition to him, but at that time, there was hope for recovery through proper medication.

Before the cardiologist left the room, Mr. Rigney said, "I taught Dr. Ricky Cole—the only medical doctor I ever taught. Do you know him?" The doctor muttered a simple "No "and somewhat dismissed this conversation. When he left the room, Mr. Rigney said, "What kind of doctor is he? He doesn't even know Ricky Cole."

He then pulled back the lower part of his sheet, lifted the stump from the amputation, and declared, "I beat this. Now I can beat this heart thing." I believe he gave it his best effort, but his condition worsened as the next ten days or so progressed. Because of his age and the seriousness of his heart condition, open heart surgery was not even a viable consideration. The doctors put him on blood thinners, but they were causing other problems and had to be discontinued. There didn't seem to be another reasonable treatment for him.

One of the effects of his problems was the congestion that prevented him from speaking clearly. His speech became more and more difficult to understand.

I visited Mr. Rigney several times during his hospital stay. The Wednesday night before he died the following Sunday, he seemed to be doing a little better, but I knew his condition was severe enough that the doctor had canceled a possible hospital discharge and his admittance to a nursing home. I just didn't realize, or maybe didn't want to accept that he was in his final days.

On Thursday night, September 27, Mike, my husband, received a call from the doctor informing us that Mr. Rigney's heart was shutting down and recovery was unlikely. She stressed that we needed to understand that he was going to die soon.

I went to the hospital on Friday after school. On the way, I spoke to the doctor on the phone. She told me that Mr. Rigney's family had agreed that he would be moved to Palliative Care, and death would be within the week. She affirmed that a "true miracle" would have to occur to avoid death. When I arrived at the hospital, he was so congested that trying to understand him was exhausting him and me. I asked the nurse if she thought he would survive the night, and she assured me that while the end was in sight, it would probably be a few days. I left him knowing that I had to help Braxton move into a new house the following day, and Rigney and Jessalyn would be with him.

As planned, Rigney and Jessalyn did visit with Mr. Rigney on Saturday. He had been moved to Palliative Care by the time they arrived. He was still trying to talk but was barely understandable--as he had been when I visited the night before on Friday. Jessalyn prayed with him, and he clearly stated that he was "worn out and ready to go home." These were the only words that she and Rigney had been able to understand while they were there.

I was with Braxton helping him move into his new house when I reviewed Jessalyn's text, which read, "I think it will be sooner rather than later." With that, I knew I needed to get to the hospital, so Mike and I left right away.

When we arrived in the Palliative Care area (Mike was with me, but left shortly), we had to put on a plastic gown, gloves, and mask because Mr. Rigney had been diagnosed with shingles. I told the nurse that I was there for the duration, be it one night or a week. She asked me what I would do if it took a week, and I told her I would wait.

He tried so hard to talk to me, but I couldn't understand anything he said. I could figure out some of the things he was trying to tell me by his gestures. I did understand the word "lawyer" after I told him I had been with Braxton. He always asked me about Braxton referring to him as "The Lawyer."

He held out his ring finger, and I knew he wanted to know where the class ring was. I told him that Brenda Kay had it. I assured him that it would be placed on his finger when "this is all over," and it would stay there forever as he would be buried with it. It is my prayer that he took it to his grave. His other niece, Esther Mae, later told me that both his ring and watch were on his hand.

I could not get him to calm down. He continued trying to talk to me, but I couldn't understand what he was saying. This went on for probably several hours—I'm not sure because I lost track of time.

At one point, we called Brenda Kay, so she could say her good-byes as I knew it wouldn't be long. He couldn't hear her talking on the phone, but I did tell him what she wanted to say to him. She wanted him to know that she loved him "with all her heart." When I repeated her words to him, he slowly shook his head up and down.

As the evening progressed, I could not get him to calm down. He continued trying to talk to me. I know there were things he wanted to say to me, but I will never know what they were.

I finally told him that I thought it was time for him to rest and go on to heaven. I told him that he was the best man I knew, and he had been like a father to me and a grandfather to my children. I also told him that it had been my pleasure to take him to visit his friends over the years. I reminded him of the great things he had done for his students throughout his teaching career, and he shook his head up and down slowly.

I told him that he would soon be seeing my mama and daddy. I asked him to tell them that my boys were grown and turning out to be fine young men. After all, my mother had died before Rigney was born. He responded by shaking his head and tried to say something, so I knew he understood.

I told him I needed him to go to sleep, so we could both rest. He raised his hands toward heaven--I don't know what he was saying, but I want to believe he was letting me know he was about to enter heaven.

We had said our "good-byes" as best we could, given the circumstances. I was at peace, and I knew he was. The nurses came in and gave him a shot that put him to sleep. I was grateful that he was going to sleep, but I didn't fully realize he would never wake up. Regrettably, I then went to sleep.

I heard the nurses in the room early the next morning. His breathing had stopped, so as far as I know, he never woke up after taking the shot the night before. I don't know his exact time of death, but I was in the room with him when he breathed his final breath. My greatest regret is falling asleep and not being beside him, talking to him. The nurses assured me that he knew I was there. Oh, I sure hope he did.

I called Rigney and Jessalyn, and they immediately drove from Cornelius to say their final good-byes. Mike came from Boone and spent some final moments with him. After leaving the hospital, the four of us went to breakfast and shared many fond memories of Mr. Rigney. I am positive that my greatest favor to him was naming my baby boy after him. It is my hope that this name will be passed on through future generations of my family.

There are so many reasons why this man was special to me. Our earthly relationship began when I got my first real teaching job in Patrick

County, Virginia, in August 1984 and ended that morning on September 30, 2018.

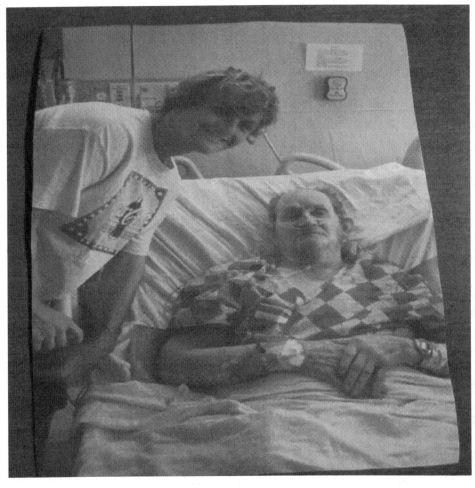

Rigney Marcela visits with Mr. Rigney one week before his death at Forsyth Memorial Hospital.

Final Respects

On October 3, 2018, Rigney, Jessalyn, Mike, and I went to what we expected to be a graveside service for Mr. Rigney. No service had been planned at all; it was just a burial. His niece had done an excellent job of choosing the bronze casket and vault, which was decorated with a plaque bearing his name, birth date, and death.

Soon after, she would have a beautiful stone placed at the head of the grave. It showed a man walking up a mountain with Christ at the top, welcoming him home. She said, "The sample stone had a man on a motorcycle, but I wanted him to be walking." So appropriate and beautiful.

As his body was being lowered, I asked Esther Mae if we could say some final words, so she asked the undertakers to stop the lowering. Through tears, Rigney thanked the people for coming and offered some heartfelt sentiments and memories. Mike and I then spoke about our relationship with Mr. Rigney and all the good things he had done for all who knew him.

I referenced the many hikes we had taken through those mountains where he was being laid to rest. We then dropped red roses on his casket, and he was lowered into the mountain earth he loved.

**Mr. Rigney's gravesite in the Rigney Family Cemetery
in Fancy Gap, Virginia.**

This send-off did not do justice to his life, so a friend, Phyllis Eastridge, and I scheduled a memorial service at Patrick County High School auditorium on October 28, 2018. It was well attended by former colleagues, many of whom we had visited, and friends.

As I prepared the program, I felt it was only appropriate that my son, Rigney, open the ceremony.

After Phyllis played "Precious Memories" on her violin, Rigney began by saying, "If Mr. Rigney is watching, he is saying, 'Ah, you've got better things to do.' I know if you are a teacher, he would say you have better things to do on a Sunday afternoon."

Through his tears, he shared his memories of driving Mr. Rigney to visit friends. While he didn't go as often as I did, there was nothing Mr. Rigney enjoyed more than showing off Rigney to his friends introducing him as "My Boy."

Rigney concluded his remarks by referencing the alpaca farm, "Be like Mr. Rigney and go see the alpacas. Take time to enjoy seeing them."

Among the speakers at his service was Dr. Joe Knight, who had been one of his first and most successful students in Patrick County. He is now an engineering professor at Duke University in Durham, North Carolina. I had heard Mr. Rigney speak of him many times as Dr. Knight had been part of the group that performed one-act plays. He remembered Mr. Rigney sponsoring this group and traveling with them to various locations where they competed many years ago. An old textbook opened to a short play entitled *The Oyster and Pearl* lay on the stage in front of Dr. Knight as he reminisced about those days.

Charles Hamm, the local owner of Hamm Family Garage in Patrick County, spoke about his experiences in Mr. Rigney's classroom. He mentioned that Mr. Rigney read aloud to the class and would stop "without missing a beat and say, 'Charles Hamm, you shut your mouth.'"

Mr. Hamm also mentioned the many times that Mr. Rigney would call him and ask him to come and get his car at the high school and work on it during the school day. He would pick the car up and have it back to him in time for his return to Fancy Gap at the end of the day. The Hamm Family Garage was one of Mr. Rigney's favorite places to visit.

I will never forget the first time he asked me to take him there. I had missed work to go to the dentist. Since my dentist's office was not far from Mr. Rigney's apartment, I went to see him and take him out for a ride. When he said he wanted to go to the Hamm Family Garage, I had no idea whom he was talking about nor where this place was located.

Three generations of the Hamm Family pictured at their garage. Charles Hamm, center, is the owner of the garage. Both Charles and his son were Mr. Rigney's students. Charles, grandson (left) currently attends PCHS.

He said it was in Stuart, Virginia, so following his directions, we arrived at the garage about fifty minutes later. I did not know anyone who worked there, so I just went into the office and explained that George Rigney was in the car and wanted to see Charles Hamm and his son, both of whom he had taught.

When I spoke his name, a busy mechanic rolled from under a car, and another one laid down his tools and walked out to my car. It seemed they all knew him and had a great conversation. There was even a very young boy, grandson of the owner, who came out to visit. He was, of course, too young to know Mr. Rigney, but they talked as though he too had been one of his students.

I took pictures of all these men with Mr. Rigney. Like all the pictures I took, they hung on his wall until his death. We would visit this family several times, and they were always as receptive and welcoming as they were that first Friday.

David Ratliff, another former student, and colleague also came from Davidson, North Carolina, and spoke at the memorial. When David was a young teacher, he was the one who nominated Mr. Rigney for the Sallie Mae Teaching Award. He not only reminisced about his days as Mr. Rigney's student and about working with him as a teacher at Patrick

County High School. David even made the statement, "I wouldn't be where I am without him."

Because David had left teaching and gone to work in the corporate world, he said, "I don't think Mr. Rigney ever forgave me for leaving teaching." It might be a slight exaggeration to say that he never forgave David, but he was sorely disappointed. He held David in very high esteem and had envisioned a great teaching career for him. David had written Mr. Rigney a letter and explained his success and satisfaction with his job with Citgo Oil Company. Mr. Rigney was indeed proud of his success but still stood by his belief that the world missed out on a good teacher.

Dr. Stewart Roberson, former student and Superintendent of the Year of Virginia Schools, spoke about his experience in Mr. Rigney's English class many years ago. He, too, had been part of the one-act playgroup that Mr. Rigney sponsored. Like Dr. Knight, he referenced the trips to these competitions.

Stewart is the son of Mr. Rigney's dear friend Dean Roberson. He further reflected on his career as an educator and the influence Mr. Rigney had on him. After being named Superintendent of the Year, Stewart had visited Mr. Rigney at the nursing home.

Left, Trey Cox, the present principal of Patrick County High School and right, James K. Hiatt, the first principal of Patrick County High School.

He remembered that when he walked into the room, Mr. Rigney said, "Stewart Robertson, is that you? Did you ever amount to anything?" Dr. Robertson was one of Mr. Rigney's prize students as he devoted his life to education.

Stuart's brother, Chip was also in attendance that day. Later in the service, when the congregation was asked to share memories, he shared his favorite Mr. Rigney's quote, "You can do it again next year." While it was a rarity for a student to fail Mr. Rigney's class, those are the words he would use when a student started to get out of line.

In addition to the students who shared memories of Mr. Rigney, there were two esteemed speakers: Mr. James K. Hiatt and Fred M. Brim, former principal and assistant principal of Patrick County High School.

Mr. Hiatt spoke first, sharing many fond memories of his years as Mr. Rigney's principal. He remembered once asking Mr. Rigney how he could get his car out of Fancy Gap mountain to the main road in the early, coldest hours of snowy mornings. Mr. Rigney asked him to come and look at something.

"He opened his trunk and showed me four tires wrapped in snow chains."

Mr. Rigney had explained, "I put these tires on the car at night when I get home. In the morning, I drive to the main road, stop, and put the unchained tires on the car."

This is just one more example of his dedication to arriving at Patrick County High School and delivering his lessons. There were many snowy mornings that he made his way to school, not knowing if conditions would allow him to return safely in the evening.

Mr. Brim, the last person he visited before his death, spoke about their visit together on September 1. He mentioned the plans they made to visit again in the spring--the visit that will not take place on this earth. Mr. Brim is such a holy man, who devoted decades of his life to education. These two men had such a major influence on each other and remained friends all those years.

There were other speakers at his service, including my son, Braxton; my husband, Mike; Ray Smith, the teacher he visited on September 1; Phyllis Eastridge, fellow English teacher; a preacher and former student, and me.

I was the final speaker, and I shared my time with Mr. Rigney on that final night at Forsyth Memorial Hospital. I also recounted the many,

many hours I spent on the road with him. I reiterated what a privilege it had been to drive him around to visit his friends.

As I faced the group assembled in the school auditorium, I saw many of the people we had visited. It was heartwarming to see that they had come to pay final respects.

I shared my memory of trying to find Gurney Royal, who was the first man that Mr. Rigney had asked me to take him to visit. Mr. Royal and his wife had visited him in the nursing home. He had also taught his children and grandchildren.

I had had a very hard time finding Mr. Royal, but finally located his grandson, who gave us directions to his home. We would visit him many times before Mr. Royal was no longer physically able to come out of the house.

Mr. Royal's son, grandson, and other members of Gurney Royal's family were among those who had come to pay their final respects. I had a good conversation with the grandson after the celebration.

When I finished speaking, Bill Rotenberry, a former high school classmate of Mr. Rigney's, sang Vince Gill's song entitled, "Go Rest High on That Mountain." Such a fitting song for this occasion.

Before the service concluded, a few people shared their memories of Mr. Rigney. I was very thankful when Dr. Rick Cole stood up to speak because, as far as Mr. Rigney was concerned, he was the only doctor who knew his craft.

While his physical body was not with us that day, his spirit will always remain at Patrick County High School. I am sure his piece of heaven looks just like his classroom.

CELEBRATION OF LIFE

GEORGE DANIEL RIGNEY
JUNE 7, 1932-SEPTEMBER 30, 2018

IN MEMORY OF GEORGE RIGNEY
--by Phyllis Eastridge

Another icon passed away,
Who touched so many souls.
For almost fifty years he manned his ship
With a black board, chalk, and a roll.

Many students came to him,
And friendship they would find.
He guided some who had lost their way;
He was firm, and helpful, and kind.

How many letters of recommendation
Were penned in his flowing style!
How many times did he enunciate
The graduates' names as they marched down the aisle!

He was first to arrive in the mornings,
And often the last to leave at night;
And at the Stop 8 Store down the road
He was a common sight.

From there he traveled forty winding miles
To his home and faithful "Wolf" in the hills of Fancy Gap,
With his bag of chips, Red Man, and a bottle of Coke
And wearing his trusty leather cap.

Not a student left his ship,
Who hadn't been taught proper grammar
From diagramming sentences,
 To the silent "t" on "often" to putting an "e" in "hammer."

At 86, his bark reached its port of call,
And there he did depart.
Another classroom awaits this humble educator,
Who has touched so many and left his mark!

Phyllis Eastridge, George Rigney, Ann Belcher, and Carroll Eastridge

Precious Memories	Performed by PHYLLIS EASTRIDGE
Welcome	RIGNEY MARCELA
Biography	MIKE MARCELA
Reflections	PHYLLIS EASTRIDGE
	BRAXTON MARCELA
Eulogy	REV. MARK LAWLESS
Reflections from former students	CHARLES HAMM
	JOE KNIGHT
	STEWART ROBERSON
	DAVID RATLIFF
Reflections	JAMES K. HIATT,
	Former Colleague
The Final Moments	MARSHA MARCELA
Musical Selection/Comments	BILL ROTENBERRY,
	Former classmate
Closing Comments/Prayer	FRED BRIM
	Former Colleague

Thank you to all who came out to celebrate the life of Mr. George Rigney. He was a true friend and leader to all of us.

Donations to the George D. Rigney Memorial Scholarship Fund can be made here today or checks can be mailed to Carter Bank at 125 E Blue Ridge Street, Stuart, VA 24171

Longtime Patrick educator died, scholarship fund to be created

George Daniel Rigney, 86, died Sept. 30 following a brief illness and hospital stay, according to Marsha Marcela, a former English teacher at Patrick County High School and one of Rigney's longtime friends.

Rigney was a teacher for 50 years and spent most of his career as an English teacher at Patrick County High School. He frequently told the story of accepting a job as a central office administrator in Patrick – a position he held for two weeks before asking to return to teaching because he wanted daily contact with students.

He never applied for another administrative position, and is remembered by many students as the last person they saw when they left school because he was on parking lot duty every day. As one of the sponsors of the senior class, he announced

(See Teacher p. 6)

224

Epilogue

You have just completed the last seven years of my journey with Mr. Rigney. Thank you for choosing to come along. Some of you were physically part of that journey, and for that, I am thankful. Many of you knew him long before I ever met him, so you may have been a bigger part of the journey than I was.

Some of you may have been on this journey with us, but not mentioned. If that is the case, please accept my apologies. I took Mr. Rigney so many places that I just couldn't give an account of all of them. Make no mistake about it, you were important to him, or he would not have opted to visit you. You may have been part of his life, but never received a visit from him. If that is the case, it is likely because I didn't know where to find you…or we just ran out of time.

As indicated in my story, many of those we visited have passed on to better places. Algie Spencer spent hours in the front seat of my car with Mr. Rigney one Sunday afternoon. They had been friends ever since Mr. Rigney arrived in Patrick County.

We made numerous visits to Beatrice Wood. She came to her kitchen door using her walker and sat on its small seat while he leaned on his walker on her carport. This was one of the few places where he was willing to get out of the car as she wasn't able to come out because of surgery. We both missed seeing her once she passed.

Jimmy Kirkman, a former principal who became a Presbyterian minister, was another friend who passed away. We visited Mr. Kirkman several times. He used a wheelchair and had to be brought out to my car for his visit. Despite his declining health and dementia, which made communication difficult, he seemed to make a connection with Mr. Rigney. Perhaps he remembered him and their time together so long ago. Mr. Kirkman's son came to Mr. Rigney's apartment to let him know about his father's death. He brought him a copy of the obituary and a family picture. We later took money to Mrs. Kirkman and asked her to purchase flowers for his grave.

During the seven years that Mr. Rigney and I traveled together, there was never a visit that was not well-received. People of all ages, occupations, and backgrounds were thrilled to see him and share memories with him.

While Mr. Rigney enjoyed his visits with former colleagues immensely, the most important people in his life, aside from his family members and my family members, were his students. We visited some as part of our drives, we randomly ran into some at various locations, and others, we never saw. That doesn't mean that he didn't talk about his memories of them.

Often during our travels, we spent much time in conversation. Since both of us were English teachers, we spent much time remembering and talking about former students whom we had shared, especially those we had taught in summer school throughout the years.

We also talked about teaching grammar in our English classes. We both loved grammar and all of its rules, and Mr. Rigney continued to be able to diagram sentences until the end.

I love grammar too, but I don't enjoy teaching it nearly as much as he did, nor do my students learn it as well as his students did. He knew I was very knowledgeable of grammar usage and writing—perhaps not to his level, but I felt quite confident with my speaking, writing, and teaching.

However, we had one recurring disagreement about the use of the words "me" and "I." While attending Appalachian State University, my grammar professor taught me that the word "than" is a preposition. Mr. Rigney argued that "than" is a conjunction. If I said, "Mr. Rigney is older than me," he argued that the proper statement would be, "Mr. Rigney is older than I."

According to my professor, the pronoun "me," would be used as an object of the prepositional phrase "than me." According to Mr. Rigney, "than" was a conjunction connecting two independent clauses: "Mr. Rigney is older" and "I [am]," with the understood verb "am."

Neither of us would give up the argument. We sometimes agreed to disagree, but he would later revisit the argument. Sometimes we agreed that either way could be correct, but he usually reneged on that too. We looked it up on the internet and learned that his way should be used in more formal conversation and writing, but my way was considered acceptable in casual conversation.

Although we never reached an agreeable conclusion about this matter, neither of us cared. This was just a small matter that would occasionally surface in our conversation. In the overall scheme of things, it makes no difference to me which one of us was right or wrong.

It was the students, teachers, family members, and adventures that filled our journey. Whatever your role in our journey, even if you were a stranger to us when you joined, I believe you will discover that there are no three people more eccentric than Mr. Rigney, Rigney, and me (…or is it "I)."

Scholarship Fund

To keep his memory alive, The George Daniel Rigney Scholarship Fund was created. People donated money at the memorial service, and others sent checks to the bank. The first scholarship was given to Hannah Roberson at PCHS in May 2019. Another scholarship was awarded to Miranda Cox in May 2020 and, hopefully, for many more in years to come.

Once the memorial service and the establishment of the scholarship fund were announced in local newspapers, I received the following email from one of Mr. Rigney's former students:

> "My husband, Tim, and I both had Mr. Rigney at PCHS. I wanted to share this with you.
> One day Mr. Rigney asked my husband, Tim Lyon, what his plans were after graduation. Tim told him he planned to attend DCC. Mr. Rigney said this, 'I wrote a recommendation for a guy last year, and he received a scholarship to DCC....and I'm going to do that for you, too.' And he did. My husband received a full scholarship to Danville Community College because of George Rigney. What an awesome gift he gave to Tim that has truly benefited our family.
>
> He also loved to tease Tim and me about dating. We have been married
>
> for almost 29 years now .
>
> I wish that we could attend the service. We were home visiting family last weekend, and my husband has to teach Sunday School on Sunday. Thank you for honoring such a wonderful human being!!"

The email was followed later by a generous donation to the scholarship fund. Tim graduated from PCHS in 1984 and earned an Associate degree in Electrical Engineering from Danville Community College. His wife, Christina, graduated in 1986. Both fondly remember Mr. Rigney and appreciate his influence on their lives.

Tim and Christina Lyon at their Junior/Senior Prom at PCHS

Both my sons received the following Facebook message from Robert, another former student following the memorial service:

> "Just want to say…Thank you for the words today…about Mr. G. Rigney. I had Mr. Rigney for my senior year. It was 'good times'…Class of '89. Thank you.

It is these types of testimonies from former students that make a scholarship fund all the more important. He has touched the lives of so many students, and the scholarship will allow him to continue to touch lives even now that he has departed.

When I presented the first scholarship in May 2019 in the PCHS auditorium, I announced that I was presenting the first-ever George D. Rigney scholarship, and there was tremendous applause. I then spoke the following words:

"On September 30, 2018, George Rigney, one of PCHS's greatest teachers, gave up his fight. As I look around this auditorium, I see many people who were likely taught by Mr. Rigney. If you were not one of his students, you might be saying, "He taught my mother, father, even my grandmother or grandfather. No doubt, he taught someone you know if you are from this area.

Some of you young men may have had your name announced by him when you graduated—with each syllable having been perfectly enunciated.

(When I said that many of the men in the audience looked around and smiled at each other or laughed.)

Every year at this time, Mr. Rigney could be found in his room, typing recommendations for his students who were hoping to get scholarships. To keep his spirit and name alive at this place he loved so much, we established this scholarship in his name. It is my goal that his name remains a household word throughout Patrick County for years to come.

The recipient of this scholarship is to be a first-generation college student like he was, a scholar like he was, and someone who stands out and contributes to the community--like he did. It appears that we found this student. The recipient of this scholarship is an officer of the Student Government, a star member of the girls' basketball team, and a volunteer in her church and community. It is her goal to do mission work and make the world a better place through her talents.

Her essay says that she plans to pursue a career in dentistry. If this dream is to come to fruition, she will be in school for many years. It will take much hard work and perseverance. When it seems to be too much, I hope she will remember that it took Mr. Rigney ten summers to earn his bachelor's degree. He worked full-time in unaccredited schools throughout the school year and attended summer classes. He paid his way and had to get car rides with other students from his area or ride a bus to get to Radford University. He not only reached his goal but helped others reach their goal.

It is my hope that Hannah Roberson will face the world with the same determination that he did. Please accept this award in his name and use it wisely."

It is my hope that this scholarship will continue for many years to come. Proceeds from the sale of this book will help maintain this scholarship.

Patrick County High School

SENIOR HONORS BANQUET & SCHOLARSHIP CEREMONY

MAY 16, 2019

Marsha Marcela

About The Author

Marsha Marcela, a native of Mount Airy, North Carolina, currently lives in the beautiful Blue Ridge Mountains in Vilas, North Carolina, with her husband, Mike. After receiving her bachelor's degree in English, she began her career at Patrick County High School, where she taught for fourteen years. She then taught for twenty years in North Carolina Public Schools retiring in 2018 and currently teaches language arts at Johnson County Middle School in Mountain City, Tennessee.

She has a growing interest in tourism and is employed part-time at The Blowing Rock Attraction in Blowing Rock, North Carolina. She and her husband also appear at Tweetsie Railroad in November and December as Mr. and Mrs. Santa Claus. Marsha continues to be passionate about her teaching career as well as her work at tourist attractions.

Her greatest accomplishments are her two boys and their significant others: Braxton and his fiancée, Kristen McDowell, and Rigney and his lovely wife, Jessalyn.

George D. Rigney

George D. Rigney teaches English 12 and Sociology. He has a B. S. and M. S. from Radford College. His hobbies are collecting teaching materials.

Mr. Rigney signed Tom Perry's senior annual.

Publisher's After Thought

"I went to school with your daddy." Whenever I entered Room 124 across from the hall from the cafeteria at Patrick County High School, where I graduated, I was greeted by George Rigney the same way. My father drove to Radford College with George Rigney when they were completing their Master's degrees in the early 1960s. Mr. Rigney always reminded me of that when I would pop my head into his classroom to talk before I headed back to class after lunch.

I never had George Rigney as a teacher, but I had him as a friend. You never knew what he was going to say or what he would be wearing. His combination of plaids and stripes was legendary, but there was so much more to him than his eccentric clothing choices. My father remembers him well standing at the back of the classroom as he taught *Macbeth* to his students. Most of us remember him teaching the art of diagramming sentences at the chalkboard.

As I walked across the stage to accept my diploma George Rigney announced "Thomas David Perry" with that emphasis we all remember so well when we were Patrick County Cougars. He announced us to all the world.

I thank you for purchasing this book to raise money for a scholarship in his name so that his legend will live on for those of us who knew him and to help educate future generations.

Thomas David "Tom" Perry

Publisher

Patrick County High School Class of 1979

Members of the Literary Staff are: Front Row (left to right): Denise Coalson, Pam Hopkins, and Tommy Inman. Second Row: Mr. Rigney (Advisor), Sandra Clark, Judy Larson, Leslie Shelor, and Ricky Fain.

From Tom Perry's 1979 Patrick County High School Annual.

There was so much more to George Rigney than his unusual clothes choices.

George D. Rigney teaches English 12 and Sociology. He has a BS and an MS from Radford College.

ISBN: 9798649069717

Copyright 2020 Marsha Marcela

This book published by agreement with

Tom Perry's Laurel Hill Publishing

**Tom Perry's
Laurel Hill Publishing**

BEYOND
MAYBERRY

Thomas D. "Tom" Perry
4443 Ararat Highway
P O Box 11
Ararat VA 24053

276-692-5300
laurelhillpub@gmail.com
https://squareup.com/store/
laurel-hill-publishing-llc

Autographed copies available at https://
squareup.com/store/laurel-hill-publishing-llc
and
Available Tom Perry's Author Page on
Amazon at https://www.amazon.com/-/e/
B002F4UJGEA

Made in the USA
Columbia, SC
02 September 2020

19111285R00133